Mexico

An Expat's Guide

Mexican Expat Immigration, Housing and Living Options,
Work & Business, Family & Education, Retirement,
Relocation Tips, Taxes & Banking, Essential Expat Guide
and Much More!

By Tess Downey

Foreword

Why Move In To Mexico?

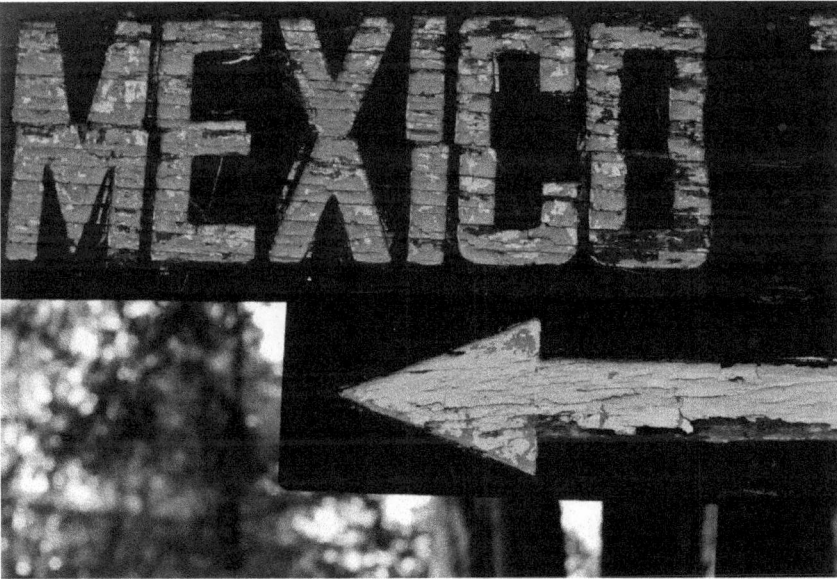

That is the simple question you have to answer. In fact, that is the *only* question you need to answer.

You may have different reasons as to why you wanted to live in this beautiful country for good or for a period of time but whatever it may be, your 'why' should be very strong, very deliberate, and very intentional to the degree where you would be willing to trade your home country or birthplace and the right of becoming a first class citizen in exchange for something that you're not entirely familiar with, but could possibly give you a new outlook or better opportunities in life. Your 'why' shouldn't be "surface – level answers," you know, something like the following:

Why Do You Want to Live in Mexico?

- "I visited Mexico last month, it was great! The people are great, the food is great, and the landmarks are fantastic! I think I want to live there."
- "I'm bored here in my hometown, I think I want to go live in a new country, hey what about Mexico?"
- "All my friends are now expats in Mexico, they said it was great living there, I wanted to try it out."

If you notice, those reasons or "whys" are considered surface – level because it's something that is out of your control, and not truly a personal reason. It's something that only your friends recommended, it's something that you decided out of boredom, it's something that just came into mind, and it's something that depended entirely on the people or food or great places of a particular country.

Of course, there's nothing wrong with those reasons but it's definitely not something that will convince you to *stay* when things get tough – and at some point, it will. If living in your own country already presents challenges, what more in a foreign land – with a different language, different culture, different upbringing, and different way of living?

You have to keep in mind that you're not just going to travel to Mexico as a tourist; you're going to live there AS IF you're a Mexican, as if you're one of them. If moving into another state is already tough for you, immigrating into another country is absolutely a tougher and different ball game. After all, you won't stay here for just a while, becoming an expat means you're going to stay here for a *long* while or for life.

If you're planning of moving in to another country, it's not just about you transferring your stuff to other places or becoming a resident in a foreign place, it's definitely you leaving your whole life behind and uprooting or perhaps rebooting your entire life. The decision of moving in to another country, probably changing citizenship along the way, and living there for quite some time (or forever) is undoubtedly a huge undertaking and will need lots of commitment on your part, simply because it will change your life.

Anything that is possibly "life – changing" should be taken seriously and should be given a LOT of thought. You should take your time, consider everything – the good, the bad, and the ugly as well as consult with people in your life that could be affected by this decision. It's like getting married so to speak.

The course of your life will definitely change, it doesn't matter what age you are, what your purpose is, your financial capacity, how long you're going to stay, who you're going with or what you're planning to do, it can all change. You never know what could happen; you never know how the country, its people, culture, and overall way of living can change you. You never know what kind of values, beliefs, and habits you are going to adapt – and if those things will make you a better or worse person in the end.

You will not just leave your home country, you'll also leave your friends and family behind, you'll leave existing opportunities, you'll leave a huge chunk of your life, and pretty much leave everything that made you who you are.

This is the reason why you should know your main purpose, your main goal or perhaps something that you would want to achieve in the end or for the time being because a lot is at stake here. If you don't have a strong 'why,' you'll not just waste your time, money and effort, you'll also end up miserable – miserable in a country that you cannot really claim as your own.

You will have a new kind of experience for sure, you'll become a slightly different person, you'll have new set of friends and new sets of relationships, you'll have different opportunities, and you'll have a fresh take in life because you'll see it through the eyes of a Mexican as you become one of them.

Do you want to live here to learn? Learn what? Do you want to live here because of work? What's in it for you? Do you want to live here for fun? What kind of "fun" do you want to experience? Do you want to settle here because this is the place you want to retire in? Do you want to live here because the cost of living is much better than your home country? Do you want to live here because this is where you want to raise your kids? Why? What's your big and unshakable 'why' – that no amount of tragedy or threat or hardship will make you pack up your bags and take the next flight back to where you came from?

You have to be specific; you have to make up your mind as to what you want to do once you live here, and you have to stand firm in your decision that no matter what, Mexico is now the place you want to call 'home.'

Table of Contents

Mexico as Your New 'Home'

Deciding to live in Mexico or any country for this matter will take lots of planning, research, knowledge, and commitment if you really wanted to live the expat life. Organizing your resources before, during, and after you moved in will make you exhausted for sure, especially if you're going to move there with your whole family because you will need to literally file everything for everyone, and of course, consider all their needs in order to make the transition as smooth as possible.

It's highly recommended that you and your family take a trip to Mexico (again, if you've been there already) before planning the nitty gritty details on how to settle in this colorful country, just to let the thought of living there sink in and sort of get into your head.

Most travellers or expats suggest that you should live in the city for quite some time or even for a longer period, say like 3 to 6 months if you can, before deciding to become a resident, in order to make sure that you're not just making any impulse decisions, and to also gauge if you can quickly adjust to your new environment or simply get used to the new lifestyle. Most people who are planning to live in Mexico temporarily or even permanently are usually travelling to different states for months up to a year or so, and even renting houses to find a place that feels right for them or to become familiar to the Mexican way of life.

You'll never know what it would feel like to live in Mexico until you do. Again, there's a huge difference in just travelling to the city for a brief period of time and actually living there. The problem with most expat newbies or prospecting foreigners is that they underestimate the time and effort it will take in adapting to a new living environment, dealing with the possibility of being homesick, and that feeling of 'belongingness.'

There are a lot of successful expat stories wherein they went to Mexico once or twice, "fell in love" with the city, and then decided to live there. It might work for some people who are probably young and looking for an adventure or someone who is nearing retirement and are looking for a new place to experience, but of course, not everyone can immediately commit to this kind of undertaking or have the luxury to pursue it.

The length and purpose of your stay will definitely affect your choices especially in terms of accommodations. If you're not planning to become a resident, then perhaps renting a house is ideal, otherwise buying a property might be a better choice since it's for long term. If you're going to live in Mexico for work or business purposes, then what you need to decide on is how long you're going to keep that job or run your business. Your main purpose of moving here could be temporary, but you still need to prepare for the possibility of you settling in the country permanently. This scenario happens to most foreigners working there; that even after their contract ended, they eventually decided to live in the country for good. Some people have no choice but to become a permanent resident because they're marrying a Mexican or another expat already living there. Whatever the reason may be, it's always recommended that you get to know the city and its people first so that you can make plans accordingly.

The chapters and sections here in this book highlights some of the most important factors you and your family should consider as you make plans and decide on your move. The topics here will present both the advantages and disadvantages of principal aspects in becoming an expat in Mexico so that you can assess and evaluate things out and be able to make informed decisions.

This book will also provide you a wealth of knowledge about what you can expect in this beautiful country once you live here, how you can stay grounded, enjoy your time, and absorb the amazing Mexican culture so that you can have successful move to these vibrant country.

Of course, this book may not be able to cover every single detail, you'll get all the basic information you need in becoming an expat but the rest is up to you. Consider it a form of exploration; as if you're a foreigner from a faraway land who had just discovered a new territory – because in a way, you are!

Keep exploring. Keep learning. Keep living.

Welcome to Mexico!

Chapter One: A Taste of Mexico

Through its rich, vibrant, and colorful history, Mexico became one of the most popular countries in Latin America. Its Native American and Spanish heritage is what makes this country unique and full of life! This chapter will give you a snapshot of what's it like living in Mexico. You'll also learn the kinds of people and expats you're going to encounter, common reasons why foreigners settle here, the cultural differences and norms you need to be aware of, and how you can deal with language barriers.

You will also be provided with a brief timeline of Mexico's history, some quick and important facts about the country as well as a preview of the basic essentials you'll need both for travelling and settling in. Are you ready to take a glimpse of this beautiful country? Read on!

Mexico in Focus

Mexico is a country known not just for its bustling metropolis but also for its cactus – studded deserts, tropical rainforests, beaches and blue waters, naturally crafted terrains, volcanoes and canyons, and of course it's flavorful nachos, tacos and hard shot tequilas!

Mexico was originally inhabited by the Mayan and Aztec civilizations before being conquered by Spanish Conquistadors. Despite suffering from the destructive forces of many colonial rulers, rebellions, civil wars, dictatorships, and natural tragedies, the country and its people has remained warm, friendly, and even maintained its vibrancy through embracing its origins, history, and rich heritage.

The countryside in Mexico is not yet 'exploited' by man – made developments which is why many people love staying here to enjoy the natural surroundings that the country can offer, on the other hand, its modern – day cities possess a unique style of architecture – one wherein you can truly distinguish its native roots.

The long history of the country is still reflected today in its rural villages, ports, mining towns, and city – center. You can still visit the Mayan temples that stood the test of time, and many preserved historical sites where you can find the ruins of the Aztec civilization that built this country thousands of years ago.

Mexico boasts many fascinating aspects that any (potential) expats will surely enjoy. You will definitely get the best of both worlds as soon as you step in this beautiful place. You'll immediately see the blend of traditional and modern – day Mexico in everything including its European - styled structures, its uniquely flavored Mexican cuisine, its very warm people, its religion, its landmarks, its colorful events and fiestas, and its overall welcoming vibe.

A Brief History of Mexico

If you want to truly enjoy living here, and appreciate more its society, culture and tradition then it is best that you have a background of what went down in history that made this country what it is today. Here's a brief timeline of Mexico:

- 1400 BCE: Development of Olmec Civilization
- 1000 BCE: Development of Mayan civilization
- 100 BCE: Mayans began building pyramids and temples
- 1000 CE: Beginning of the end for the Mayan civilization
- 1200 CE: Development of the Aztec civilization
- 1325 CE: Establishment of Tenochtitlan by the Aztecs.
- 1440 CE: Expansion of the Aztec Empire
- 1517: Hernandez de Cordoba reached the shores of Mexico
- 1519: Hernandez Cortez killed the leader of the Aztecs in Tenochtitlan
- 1521: Cortez conquered the Aztecs and the capital in Tenochtitlan

- 1600s: Spain officially conquered the rest of Mexico; arrival of Spanish settlers

- 1810: Catholic priest Miguel Hidalgo led a war of independence for Mexico against the Spaniards

- 1811: Hidalgo was executed by the Spaniards

- 1821: Mexico won the war and officially declared its independence on September 27 1821.

- 1822: Mexico assigned Agustin de Iturbide as their first Emperor.

- 1824: Mexico was turned into a republic; Guadalupe Victoria is elected as the first President of Mexico.

- 1835: Beginning of Texas Revolution.

- 1836: Texas defeated the Mexican army and declared its independence from Mexico.

- 1846: Beginning of Mexican – American war

- 1847: US Army occupied Mexico

- 1848: USA acquired new territory as the Mexican – American War ended. California, New Mexico, Utah, Nevada, Arizona, Texas officially became part of United States.

- 1861: French army invades Mexico

- 1867: Benito Jaurez defeated the French forces and eventually becomes president.

- 1910: Emiliano Zapata led the Mexican Revolution

- 1917: Adoption of Mexican Constitution

- 1923: Poncho Villa, a revolutionary leader, is assassinated.

- 1929: Establishment of The National Mexican Party which was later renamed as Institutional Revolutionary Party (PRI).

- 1930: Mexico's economy is booming

- 1942: World War II breaks out; Mexico joined forced with the Allies to defeat the Axis powers.

- 1993: Ratification of The North American Trade Agreement (NAFTA)

- 2000: Election of non – PRI party Vicente Fox as Mexican president – a first for the country in 71 years.

Reasons why People Move to Mexico

Believe it or not, most people who decided to make Mexico their new home didn't come here because of all the things mentioned earlier, well, of course all those reasons are part of it – the awesome landmarks, the beautiful culture, and the likes – but for most people it's either for professional purposes and/or personal purposes, not just the surface – level reasons I talked about in the beginning of this book. That's perhaps the main difference between being a traveller and being an expat. Travellers go here to experience everything, every "big and obvious" thing in an instant because they only have a few weeks to spare. Expats, on the other hand, live here to *immerse*, to truly be among the people, or perhaps to become something more.

Here are some of the most common reasons or themes of why foreigners, especially Americans, Europeans and Canadians decided to stay in Mexico as an expat:

- Gain access to a different way of living, experience new cultures and immerse oneself in it.
- To engage in a much relax or slow pace of living
- Due to a better climate wherein one can truly enjoy the outdoors, reconnect with nature and also promote good health.
- Desire of learning new language, new customs, and develop new relationships

- Some people want to raise their kids here because of the good moral values and beliefs that the country possesses.

- Some go here for professional purposes – either their company relocated them to Mexico to have a cross – cultural working experience while others set up their businesses here to serve a new market.

- To live a simpler lifestyle or have a reflective journey – away from the hustle and bustle in their home country.

- To maximize more their earnings as the economy here is probably much better than in their home country.

- To retire and settle in a place in order to gain new perspective and a fresh take of life.

What Is It Like as an Expat in Mexico?

The way of living in Mexico will be very different than living in your home country especially if you're from USA, Europe, and Asia since there'll be a huge cultural gap.

This section will give you a quick snapshot of what to expect once you moved here.

- **English is widely spoken but learning Spanish will go a long way.** Many establishments and people in Mexico understand English and also know how to speak the language especially if you decided to stay in an expatriate city. But of course, the common and everyday language Mexicans will use is their native tongue which is why it's highly recommended that you learn basic Spanish so you can deal with your everyday life with much ease. We'll discuss more about dealing with language barriers in the next few sections.

- **All your needs are covered.** Actually even your 'wants' are pretty much covered too unless of course you decided to stay in a very remote area. Whatever you have in your home country can also be found in Mexico including local and international restaurants, supermarkets, malls, entertainment amenities, accessible transportation, communication services etc.

- **Mexico has a slower and more relax pace of life.** Compared to countries like USA, UK, Canada, China, and the likes, Mexico is a country where people are taking their time leisurely, which is why tourists and expats love coming here to take a breather from their very busy lives back home.

- **The people are very welcoming; you won't have a hard time adjusting to them or perhaps their culture.** Of course this depends on how open you are going to be with everyone around you, generally though Mexicans are hospitable and loves to make friends with expats because they are also curious as to what life is like in other countries. It's all a matter of being open – minded and of integrating yourself in their way of life. They will appreciate you for trying and you'll eventually feel more at home if you learn how to truly connect with the locals.

- **Expat communities will make you feel at home.** Many expats choose to stay in a community where fellow expats or fellow countrymen also live. This is highly recommended because you can short – circuit the whole "adjusting and adopting process." Since these expats have lived there longer than you, for sure, they already know the ins and outs of the city, they already know some of the locals around the neighborhood, they already know some lifestyle "hacks" of where to get this, how to get there, how to do this, when to approach people, the do's and don'ts etc. They can already teach you what you need to know, introduce you to the local and expat community, and make the transition for you and your family not just smooth but also a great experience. You'll already have your own "expat lifestyle tour guide" so to speak, plus you won't suffer from the possibility of being homesick.

Mexican Culture and Norms

Mexico's culture is mostly based around family, religion, and people. They are very proud of their heritage and also patriotic. Family is the main center of Mexico's culture, once you've spent some time here, you'll notice that Mexicans love to hang out not just with their immediate families but also their third or fourth generation relatives. You'll eventually get used to the idea that they meet regularly with their loved ones as if there's always a big event or family occasion.

Even when people get married, they tend to stay or move in with their parents or in - laws, and not the other way around. That's how important family is to them; you'll find them living in close proximity to one another. Everyone is expected to contribute to the family, and the needs of the family are more important than that of an individual. The males are the decision – makers but other members may be consulted. The father is expected to provide for the family while the mother is expected to be the head of the household and take care of the children. The extended family can be asked for support financially when times get tough.

Mexicans are also very religious people; 90% of Mexicans are Catholics, and the rest are Protestants. This is another aspect of their culture that you will immediately notice as soon as you arrive in the country. Their faith is shown in almost everything they do. And compared to western culture, Mexicans' faith and belief in a higher power is almost fatalistic, this is because of the Spanish influence that brought the religion of Christianity in the country.

Many people go to church, observe Christian feasts or religious events, have crucifix and sacred images displayed in their homes, cars, public buildings, transportations, workplace etc. And because of this kind of religious upbringing, some people tend to be uptight as well. Society tolerates other religion and respect other people's way of worship so you can be sure to fully embrace your faith without being reprised.

Mexicans are also more traditional especially in terms of image and status. People who have professional titles or those with a degree are sort of being looked up to as well as people who have a high position in the corporate world or in the government.

When it comes to commitment, Mexicans know how to make promises but it may not always be delivered or done in a way you would expect. Since their culture is more laid back, they tend to sometimes fail in efficiency and punctuality. You have to remember that they are not entirely a consumer – driven, fast – paced kind of society.

They take their time in doing something; you might also encounter a lot of instances of delays or "excuses" especially in terms of work (e.g. fiestas, dead relatives, incomplete tasks etc.), and this could be sometimes frustrating especially if you grew up in a country where everything gets done as soon as possible. It may be a culture shock to some foreigners but as an expat, you have no choice but to accept it. Here are some norms you need to keep in mind if you're going to live in Mexico:

Rules of Greeting:

- Mexicans likes to greet each other through kissing the right cheek. It doesn't matter if they are friends or only casual acquaintances. However, this is only done woman to woman, and woman to man but not man to man – shaking hands is usually how two men greet each other.
- Women usually make the first move when it comes to kissing a man especially if it's a new acquaintance.

Rules of Eating:

- Whenever you find yourself dining at a restaurant, it is normal for locals to say enjoy your meal or "provecho" as they leave. Just reply thank you or "gracias" to show politeness.

Rules of Communication:

- Mexicans will usually respond in a way that will not disappoint you. Needless to say, even if the truth is unappealing they will still somehow give you a positive response because they don't want to say it like it is compared to western culture where everything is said in a direct manner. For example, if your work is not excellent, they will not directly say that it's crap or it's bad. They will tell it in a polite manner where your feelings aren't hurt that much.

- Some expats have trouble dealing with this kind of behavior or norm especially in doing negotiations in terms of business or work. They may say that they will deliver something just to assure you that everything's fine but may not always deliver. If you quickly get a positive answer, it's probably best to get other people's opinions about it especially when dealing with important matters.

Rules of Bureaucracy:

- If you're going to deal with any legal matters like purchasing a property, acquiring documents, applying for something or even opening a bank account, you will need to deal with a lot of paperwork, stamps, fees, and requirements.

- You will most probably have to wait for a period of time before getting anything done. What most expats do is that they keep multiple copies of documents they will need in the future to avoid the hassle of dealing with the long process.

Dos and Don'ts

- Don't address a person by his or her first name. This is particularly for people older than you or people you do not know because that is a sign of disrespect; unless of course you are given permission or you're already close to the person. You have to address a person by adding Mr/Ms/Mrs or Señor (male), Señora (married female), or Señorita (unmarried female).

- Don't directly point at a person because that is considered rude.

- Whenever you're shaking hands with a man or a woman, do try to always start with the oldest person (if for example, you are introduced to a family).

Speaking the Native Tongue

Mexico is a Spanish – speaking nation. As mentioned earlier, lots of Mexicans know how to speak in English for tourism purposes but many of them are still not fluent or may not entirely understand the language. This is why learning basic Spanish is very important, it will simply make your life easier, and you'll learn how to connect more with the locals.

What most expats do before going to Mexico is take a short language course so that they know how to properly greet, approach, respond or ask someone once they move to the country. Some expats who live in Mexican states where most English – speaking foreigners reside or those who work in companies that are only catering to English –

Chapter One: A Taste of Mexico

speaking customers or colleagues may not need to learn the language but the farther you are from these expatriate places, the more you need to learn the language otherwise, day to day living will be hard for you.

A little Spanish will go a long way especially if you're dealing with important or private matters. Learning a new language is also a sign of respect and politeness, you may not be perfectly fluent but the locals will surely appreciate you in making the effort to communicate or connect with them through their native tongue.

If you know how to communicate and speak their native language, you can immediately feel a sense of belongingness, make friends easily, understand basic instructions or commands, and also not get scammed or fooled by anyone. You will also have a deeper understanding of their culture and be able to truly integrate your life with the locals.

According to a language expert who teaches expats, there are two ways you can learn a language – either you learn it formally through taking up Spanish courses or you learn it informally through immersion but either way,

An Expat's Guide to Mexico   P a g e | 25

practicing and speaking it every day will make all the difference. Don't be afraid to try and fail or look like a fool at first because that's how you'll get better, in fact, that's the only way to test if you're learning the language. So just go out there, learn as much as you can, fail at it, and you'll soon find yourself already speaking like one of them Mexicans!

Chapter Two: Immigration

Now that you have been given an overview about the vibrant culture and history of Mexico, and what to expect there as you move, it's time to learn about the immigration policies, laws, and general legal requirements that you'll need to be able to reside in the country, whether you're planning to stay temporarily or permanently. This is the very first step you need to do before even planning where you're going to stay or researching about other expat essentials. The processing of papers and filing of documents that are needed for you to make a smooth transition will definitely take quite a period of time, energy, and money which is why this is a very crucial step. Once you're approved and ready to go, everything will be quite easier.

Some details may not be covered particularly for people who may have problems with their visas, passports or any other related citizenship issues, so it's up to you to consult with proper authorities in order to resolve that. You would want to make sure that everything is approved and documented properly so as not to have the possibility of being deported or have problems down the road once you've completely moved in.

This chapter will provide you with the basic and general guidelines on how to become an immigrant in Mexico including how to acquire Mexican visas for permanent and non – permanent residents, necessary permits, and summary of policies, laws, and citizenship details.

Immigration Policies

This section will give you a general overview and summary of how the Mexican immigration system works and the options available for people who are planning in visiting or moving to Mexico whether it is for professional or personal purposes including those who wanted to become a permanent resident. Mexico has a statutory and legal immigration policy under the General Law of Population that must be adhere by foreign citizens or anything that is associated with citizenship status and foreign immigration.

Two Types of Immigration Permits

There are generally two types of immigration permits in Mexico these are the following:

- **Non – Immigrant Permit** – this is a requirement for foreigners who wanted to visit Mexico for only a period of time or for a specific purpose only. (Ex: tourists, business – related meetings, temporary expats, overseas workers etc.)

- **Immigrant Permit** – this is a requirement for foreigners who wanted to stay in Mexico for a longer period or for those who wanted to acquire temporary/permanent residence in Mexico. (Ex: permanent expats, overseas workers with a long – term contract, business owners, etc.)

Acquiring Non – Immigrant Mexican Visas

The three main non – immigrant classifications for Mexican visas/permits, these are the following:

- **Visitante Permit (Visitor's Permit)** – this is not a formal visa but only a form that is intended for tourists or short – term visits only.

- **Mexican Tourist Visa** – this is particularly for foreigners/tourists from countries that are not included in the no – visa policy of Mexico.

- **Visa de Residente Temporal (Temporary Resident Visa)** – this visa is intended for foreigners who are planning to stay in Mexico for not more than 4 years.

Visitante Permit (FMM)

The Visitor's Permit is issued for people who are only planning to visit Mexico for personal, professional or leisure purposes within only 6 months. The Visitor's Permit will be given to you once you arrive in Mexico either by air or by land (if you travel beyond the so - called 'free border zone' or beyond the 35 km free zone).

You'll need to fill up a form called Forma Migratoria Multiple (FMM) which is given by airlines before landing. It is also available at international/local airports, and is issued at different entry ports (land/sea). This permit is only valid for up to 180 days (6 months) and it is neither renewable nor transferrable. If you wanted to extend your stay (beyond 180 days), you need to visit the office of immigration or any immigration centers at the airport to pay a fine before leaving the country. The penalty will depend on how long you overstayed per day. If ever you lost your FMM then make sure to arrange it and apply for a replacement a few days before leaving the country so as not to miss your scheduled flight. You'll need to pay, at the time of this writing, US$30 for your visitor's permit to be replaced.

As with all immigration policies, whether your country is included in the no – visa list or not, you'll need to have a passport that is valid for 6 months. You will also need to leave the country once the visitor's permit has expired. If you don't apply for your permit to be extended or any temporary/resident visas, you will be deemed illegal or undocumented, and may have to face a penalty, prison time or even deportation.

Here are the countries that do not need to apply for a formal tourist visa, you'll only need a passport (w/ 6 months of validity), FMM, and travel documents (ex: hotel reservation, tour tickets, return tickets, letter of invitation (if invited by any relatives/organizations, working contract etc.)

- American Samoa
- Andorra
- Anguilla
- Argentina
- Aruba
- Australia
- Austria
- Azores Islands
- Bahamas (Comonwealth)
- Barbados
- Belgium
- Belize
- Bermuda

- British Indian Ocean Territory
- British Virgin Islands
- Bulgaria
- Canada
- Cayman Islands
- Chile
- Christmas Islands
- Cocos Islands
- Cook Islands
- Costa Rica
- Cyprus
- Czech Republic
- Denmark
- Estonia
- Falkland Islands
- Faroe Islands
- Finland
- France
- French Guiana
- French Polynesia

- Germany
- Gibraltar
- Greece
- Greenland
- Guadalupe
- Guam Islands
- Hong Kong (People's Republic of China)
- Hungary
- Iceland
- Ireland
- Israel
- Italy
- Japan
- Latvia
- Liechtenstein
- Lithuania
- Luxembourg
- Macao (People's Republic of China)
- Malta

- Marianas Islands
- Marshall Islands
- Martinique
- Mayotte
- Micronesia
- Monaco
- Montserrat
- Netherlands Antilles
- Netherlands (Holland)
- New Caledonia
- New Zealand
- Niue Islands
- Norfolk Islands
- Norway
- Palau
- Panama
- Paraguay
- Pitcairn Islands
- Poland
- Portugal
- Puerto Rico
- Reunion
- Romania
- San Marino
- Santa Helena
- Singapore
- Slovakia
- Slovenia
- South Korea
- Spain
- Sweden
- Switzerland
- Tokelau
- Trinidad and Tobago
- Turks and Caicos
- United Kingdom of Great Britain
- United States of America
- Unites States Virgin Islands

- Uruguay
- Venezuela

- Wallis and Futuna Islands

Mexican Tourist Visa

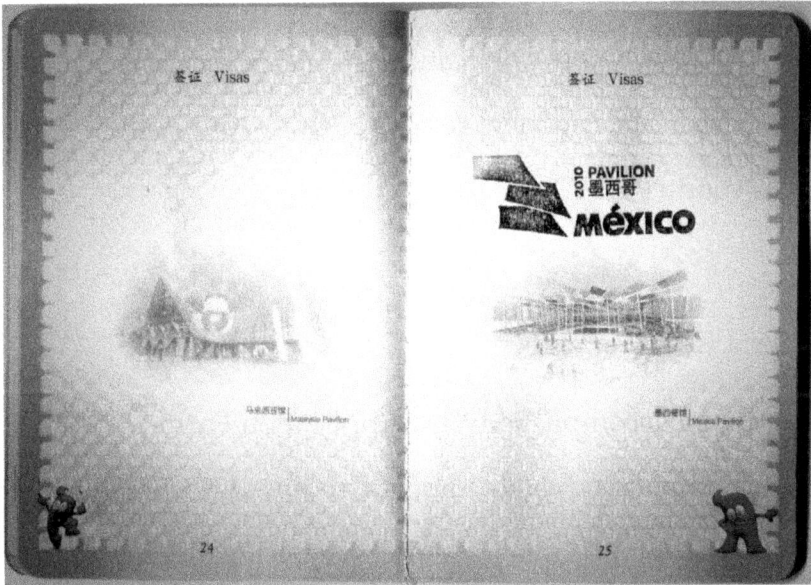

Obviously, if your country is not exempted or not listed in the no – visa policy of the immigrations, then that means you should apply for a formal Mexican tourist visa. Here's how to know if you are eligible:

- You should have a valid passport (valid for 6 months)
- Duly accomplished visa application form
- Proof of financial ability (ex: bank account, return tickets, hotel reservations, work/business contracts

etc). The Mexican Immigration requires travellers to at least have US$50 per day budget for the duration of your trip.

- Round trip ticket
- Formal bank statement from your bank for the last 6 months before application
- Proof of permanent residence from your home country

General Requirements:

- Duly accomplished Visa Application Form
- Complete travel documents/ required documents
- Photographs that have proper specifications in your visa application and passport
- Paid Visa Application Fee

Some Reminders:

- After submitting your requirements and paying for the application fee at the nearest Mexican Embassy in your country, you just need to wait for your visa to be issued. Make sure to claim it on time. The visa fee is around US$22 at the time of this writing.

- The Mexican Tourist Visa is valid up to 6 months only, if you wanted to extend your stay; you need to apply at least 30 days or 1 month prior to your visa's expiration. You also need to show proof that you have the financial capacity to stay or proof of documents if it's for work or business purposes.

Visa de Residente Temporal (Temporary Resident Visa)

The Temporary Resident Visa is for people who wanted to live in Mexico for more than 6 months. This is different from just overstaying in the country as permitted by the FMM/ Visitor's permit or the Mexican Tourist Visa. If you wanted to become a temporary resident that means you can stay in the country more up to 4 years only. This is a renewable permit that initially has a validity of 1 year, after which you need to renew it if you wanted to stay longer up to the maximum period of 4 years.

Once issued, you will be considered a non –
immigrant with a temporary resident status. You will be
allowed to come into and from Mexico and have a right to
live in the country for 4 years under the visa's terms. The
visa will have terms that you need to follow especially in the
kinds of activities you will be engaged in whether lucrative
or non – lucrative, this will all depend on the classification of
your temporary visa. Make sure to know the specific terms
of your visa and consult an immigration officer if need be.

General Requirements:

- Duly accomplished Temporary Resident Visa
  application form
- Valid Passport, photocopies of identity and travel
  documents
- Photographs that have proper specifications in your
  visa application and passport
- Proof of investments, bank statements, permanent
  residence (if applying from overseas) etc.

- Employment papers/contracts, business permits/contracts, investment deeds, property titles etc.
- Letter of Invitation by an organization/company/school
- Matrimonial affidavits
- Other essential documents/ affidavits as specifically required by the consulate or immigration office.

Some Reminders:

- For you to be eligible for a temporary resident visa, you need to prove that you'll have sufficient funds or steady income to sustain yourself or your family for more than a year or up to 4 years. There will be financial requirements that you'll need to meet as stated in Mexico's immigration laws.

- If you apply for a temporary visa overseas, the visa will not be issued by foreign consuls, what the immigration office will do is to process your papers and pre – approve your application, after which, they will put a Visa sticker in your passport. Upon arrival in Mexico, you need to go to the immigration office within 1 month of your arrival to exchange your temporary sticker stamp for a temporary visa card.

- Once you are approved and granted a temporary resident visa, you can renew it until the 4th year. Once the 4 year period ends, you either apply for a permanent resident visa or leave the country. You cannot apply for another temporary visa anymore.

- The processing fee is around US$40 at the time of this writing.

Acquiring Immigrant Mexican Visa

The Permanent Resident Visa is given to foreign citizens who wish to stay in Mexico and settle here indefinitely or for those who wanted to become a citizen of Mexico.

Visa de Residente Permanente (Permanent Resident Visa)

You don't really need to have a Temporary Resident Visa in order to apply for a Permanent Resident Visa, you just need to complete the requirements needed for permanent residency. Below are the people eligible to apply for a permanent resident visa:

- If you have family or relatives in Mexico

- If you are a retiree but have sufficient financial capacity or monthly income (such as pension) as proof that you can support oneself.

- If you have been a temporary resident in Mexico and have stayed for four consecutive years.

- If you lived in Mexico for two consecutive years with a temporary resident status wherein the visa was issued because you married a Mexican citizen or a foreigner with permanent residency status

- If you meet the government's minimum score under the Point's System (this mostly applies to businessman, politicians, army, or investors who have helped the country one way or another).

- If you have been granted under humanitarian grounds or political asylum/

General Requirements:

- Duly accomplished Permanent Resident Visa application form
- Valid Passport, photocopies of identity and travel documents
- Photographs that have proper specifications in your visa application and passport
- Proof of investments, bank statements, permanent residence (if applying from overseas) etc.
- Employment papers/contracts, business permits/contracts, investment deeds, property titles etc.
- Letter of Invitation by an organization/company/school
- Matrimonial affidavits

- Other essential documents/ affidavits as specifically required by the consulate or immigration office

Reminder:

- Once you received the permanent residency status or immigrant status, you'll be given a card similar to that of a driver's license. Your visa will enable you to get into and from Mexico and the Mexican border just like any Mexican citizen.

Eligibility for Temporary and Permanent Residency within Mexico

Foreign nationals that are in Mexico and are currently holding only a Visitante Permit or FMM have the option to file an application for either a temporary resident visa or a permanent resident visa without the need to leave the country. Below are the people eligible to apply for either of the two visa classifications:

For foreign nationals with Visitor's permit who wanted to acquire a Temporary Resident Visa while in Mexico, you are eligible if:

- You are a legal spouse of a foreigner that has a temporary resident status or a permanent resident status.
- You are one of the parents of a foreign national who has a temporary resident status
- You are the child of a foreign national who has a temporary resident status as long as the son/daughter is below 18 years old or is still considered a minor.
- You are the child of the spouse of a foreign national who has a temporary resident status as long as the son/daughter is below 18 years old or is still considered a minor.
- You are the foreign spouse of a Mexican citizen

For foreign nationals with Visitor's permit who wanted to acquire a Permanent Resident Visa while in Mexico, you are eligible if:

- You are one of the parents of a foreign national who has a permanent resident status
- You are the child of a foreign national who has a permanent resident status as long as the son/daughter is below 18 years old
- You are the child of the spouse of a foreign national who has a permanent resident status as long as the son/daughter is below 18 years old
- You are the sibling of a foreign national who has a permanent resident status as long as the sibling is below 18 years old
- You are the child of a Mexican citizen as long as the child is below 18 years old (this only applies to child/children that are not entitled to Mexican citizenship or those who aren't born in the country.
- You are the child of the spouse of a Mexican citizen as long as you are below 18 years old

- You are the foreign parent of a child born in Mexico or a Mexican national

- You are the minor or adult sibling of a Mexican citizen (including those who are naturalized foreigners).

Some Reminders:

- If you only have a Visitor's permit, and you got a job offer at a Mexican corporation/company, the company should be the one who will process your paper for a temporary resident permit at the immigration office in Mexico. Once approved, you will need to leave the country, and go to the Mexican Embassy or Consulate in your home country where you will receive a sticker visa in your passport. When you come back to Mexico, you will need to exchange that visa/sticker for the Temporary Resident Visa card, before you become a Temporary Resident status holder.

- If you are not eligible from the criteria mentioned earlier, that means you will need to apply for a residency visa (either temporary or permanent) from your home country or countries outside Mexico. You can apply at any Mexican Embassy in any country you wish as long as your presence in that particular country is legal – if you have a tourist visa/ if you are a temporary/permanent resident holder etc.

- Once approved, the Mexican consul will issue a sticker in your passport (valid for 6 months) that can be exchanged for the actual resident card within 30 days of your entry in Mexico.

- You need to keep in mind that application for a Temporary or Permanent Resident Visa or Immigrant Visa are only for those foreigners or Mexican nationals that are eligible. Those who will not meet the qualifications and the criteria/requirements will not be permitted; it doesn't matter if you apply within Mexico or outside of the country.

Who Are the People Usually Qualified for Resident

Visas?

- Retirees
- Investors
- Professionals (Overseas worker, technical, scientific professions)
- Prominent People

Retirees

If you are a retiree who don't intend in working or earning money in Mexico, and you have sufficient funds to sustain yourself (either from pension, investments, business, or other financial sources), you can apply for a Permanent Resident Visa provided that you will pass the financial requirements and criteria.

Investors

You can apply and receive a resident permit if you have a financial capital that you are willing to invest in any industry, corporation or services in Mexico. There would also be a required investment amount to be eligible.

Professionals

If you are hired by a Mexican company as an overseas worker or have a contract you can apply to become an immigrant. If you are also a scientist or technician, and a foreign company sponsored you, the company should shoulder everything you need including all your expenses. The company will also be the one to request for a resident visa on your behalf.

Prominent People

If the person is prominent or has earned national or international prestige, he/she is eligible but the entry will be handled and processed at the Interior Ministry of Mexico.

Naturalization

Foreign nationals can be naturalized or granted a Mexican Citizenship. Some foreigners who have been granted a Permanent Residency status or those who are married to a Mexican national eventually take this road to formally become a 'Mexican.' There are many benefits of becoming a naturalized citizen because once you become a Mexican Citizen that means you are a first – class citizen. You will be entitled to vote and you will have all the privileges and rights as if you are born in Mexico. The only downside of course is that once you take this road, you will need to renounce your citizenship in your home country.

There will be a whole new set of requirements, criteria, eligibility, and process if you wanted to be naturalized. Aside from the paper works, you will also take an exam that you need to pass, and get interviewed by the Mexican consulate. The process is much easier and faster for foreigners who are married to a Mexican national. You can visit the Mexican Embassy in your home country or the Mexico Relocation Consulting Service for further information. You might also want to consult with an immigration officer/lawyer if this is something that you want to do.

When to Consult an Immigration Officer/ Lawyer

As mentioned earlier, if you're planning to become a Mexican citizen or you wanted to acquire a temporary/permanent resident visa, it's very ideal to talk consult an immigration officer/consul/lawyer especially if you have "special needs" or possible citizenship issues. Consulting professionals will be very beneficial for you or your family because they can give you expert advice and can also lay out options for you so that you can make informed choices before wasting any amount of money, time and effort in processing documents or applying for visas. Here are some of the benefits of hiring an immigration consultation firm/lawyer:

- You will have more confidence in applying for visas because you are being guided by a professional or an expert.
- The representative can process your paper on your behalf saving you lots of time and effort

- If in case you have trouble in your visa application, you'll be sure to ask the legal help of the immigration lawyer you hired

- The immigration lawyer can give you plenty of options, make you take the best route, and suggest proper course of action because he/she can properly assessed your situation and/or needs.

- You don't need to make repeated and exhausting (or sometimes confusing) trips to the embassy or immigration office unless your presence is required. Your lawyer will be right there with you to give you counsel.

- If you don't know how to speak Spanish, your lawyer or the immigration expert you hired can help you get through the application process.

- It will save you a lot of time, energy and even money especially if you have a complex situation.

- You will have a much confident and better chance of getting your application approved to either live, retire, do business or just experience Mexico.

Chapter Three: Best Expat Districts in Mexico

Thousands of foreigners move to Mexico every single year for various reasons including a much lower cost of living, better weather, less tax to pay, personal freedom and a more relax pace of life. Most expats come from the United States and Canada. In fact, Americans residing in Mexico are nearly one million already, that's according to the recent stats by the U.S. government.

Just about a decade ago, there are only more or less 200,000 American expatriates living in Mexico, and comparing it based from the statistics now, there's definitely a huge increase.

The sudden influx of American expats and foreigners from other nations alike is a good sign because that means that the country is very welcoming to people, and also accepting of other nation's culture and way of living. As a potential resident, you are in good company in choosing Mexico as your new home but before you hit the beach, drink tequilas with fellow 'amigos,' and know where the flavorful nachos and tacos are, it's ideal that you know first where you would settle in.

In this chapter, you will be given an overview of each state in Mexico where expatriates commonly live. You'll also know the pros and cons for each as well as the general cost of living. Before deciding where to rent or buy a house, make sure that the state you choose to settle in resonates with your reasons and your big 'why' so that you'll truly enjoy your stay in this amazing country.

Top Places Where Most Expats Live

Most expatriates especially Americans chose to live in the Yucatan State or the Yucatan Peninsula. The Yucatan Peninsula is composed of three states: Quintana Roo, Campeche, and Yucatan. Many foreigners find themselves settling in these places simply because it's quite distant from the hustle and bustle of the city – center. It's mostly a remote location, and also near many amazing sights in Mexico.

The usual reasons why most expats live here is because the quality of life is just amazing (since it's away from the busy streets), you'll get to explore Mexico and delve deeper in how its people live their lives. Despite of not being near the city, expats love to settle here because they get the same access to various services such as medical needs, housing needs, educational needs, and other basic necessities.

The cost of living is also much cheaper compared to the city, which is already an advantage itself because you can get to maximize your finances, and also get to enjoy many Mexican quality experiences. Of course, the real cherry on top here is that you are with fellow expats, which means you'll already have a ready – made community where you can learn a lot of stuff from, interact with and also help you adjust in your new living environment.

Campeche City

Campeche is one of the top districts in the Yucatan area where most expats want to settle in especially Europeans and those who love the colonial era. As soon as you get into the city, you'll immediately fall in love with its colonial aura since this city became one of the hubs of

Conquistadors back when Spaniards conquered Mexico. The city boasts colonial architecture, and cultural ambiance.

Campeche City will make you appreciate Mexico's rich history, and get you in touch with your fascination in colonial times. A fair warning though, you might become really fluent in Spanish once you stay here (and that's a good thing!).

Advantages:

- A small city with quite a cozy and colonial theme
- The cost of living is much less than most other 'expat states' in the Yucatan Peninsula (especially the cost of water).
- Not filled with tourists
- Has complete and basic necessities
- According to most expats, this is where you can fully experience what it's like to be one of them Mexicans.
- Ideal for foreigners who are retirees, and for temporary residents who wanted to maximize personal freedom and leisure.

Disadvantages

- Quite distant and remote
- The local airport has only limited flights
- Not a lot of expats live here compared to other states
- You may need to be quite proficient already in speaking the Spanish language because most people here doesn't know how to speak in English or can't fully understand it.

Yucatan State

Yucatan state is the largest place where most foreigners reside, and for many great reasons. The top two main districts for expats is the district of Merida, and Progresso. Other smaller towns in Yucatan State where expats stay in include Holbox Island, Valladolid, and Izamal. These states are also popular tourist spots because it has many surrounding beaches, beautiful housing projects (that are targeted to potential expats), international stores and restaurants, and it's also where many international events take place like concerts and various cultural events.

The best part is that the Yucatan state is surrounded by different districts and towns that are in close proximity to one another, making a less hassle travel time. You can expect not just expats from all over the world but also tourists. If you wanted to easily get adjusted to your new life, explore and connect with other people, then it's ideal that you settle here.

This state is best for young people who are planning to stay in Mexico for just a period of time, for families who have children or for expats who are planning to become temporary residents only. Of course, there's also a lot of expats here that settled in for the long term, but if you're a retiree or someone who wanted to get away from the usual tourist lifestyle, this may not be the best place for you.

Here are the districts and towns within Yucatan state. We'll give you a brief overview as well as the pros and cons of living in each:

Merida

- Merida is a place inhabited by thousands of expats from all over the world!

- This is also the largest area in the Yucatan State with a population of over a million people (comprising of locals, tourists, and expats).
- Merida is the hub of expats, and also offers many great neighborhoods to choose from.
- This place is where you can easily adjust because of the great support groups of expats around.

Advantages:

- A big place that is rich in history and culture
- Has a variety of housing styles you can choose from including modern houses, colonial – styled houses, art – deco homes, and Mexican – styled architecture.
- Merida has many newly developed subdivisions and neighborhoods which is why living arrangement is very convenient.
- A shopping paradise especially for American expats because there's a branch of Home Depot and Costco in this place.

- Has great access not just to basic necessities but also for other international goods

- The city is famous for its arts and culture scenes; you can get to experience Mexican traditions, dances, theaters, and other cultural exhibitions.

- Has an international airport as well as accessible bus stations if you want to go on a trip to other regions.

- You don't need a car because the transportation system is fast and reliable, and other surrounding towns/ tourist spots are only a few hours away.

Disadvantages

- Quite a hot city all year – round. You may need to install an air-condition in your house especially if you're not used to warm or humid temperatures.

- The place is mostly crowded since it's a tourist spot.

- There aren't natural surroundings or sightseeing opportunities because there are lots of establishments around

- The colonial era might easily wear you off because you'll have to deal with the larger Mexican city

- Flights to USA are limited and often times more expensive.

Progresso Area

Progresso is another state where most expats live especially for those people who wanted to have a more relaxed way of living, away from the busy city of Merida. If you wanted to live near the gulf coast or settle in small villages that are near the beaches, then this is the place for you. This place is also ideal for people who are retirees, have families, and also for temporary/ permanent expats who wanted to explore the rural areas of Mexico.

Advantages:

- If you dream of living in a beachfront house then this is the place for you! It offers many beachfront houses that are very affordable! It won't cost you an arm and a leg or a whole life worth of work unlike in other countries.

- Buying a land here is also cheap especially if you just decided to build your own style of house.

- Overlooking the refreshing scenery of Mexico's Gulf while catching some fresh fish is what this place offers. Perfect for retirees who just wanted to relax for the rest of their lives!

- It's not crowded compared to Merida, and it's a place where you can also enjoy the culture.

- It's only 30 minutes away from the city of Merida, so it's the best of both worlds.

Disadvantages:

- Quite a remote area

- The small village kind of lifestyle might easily bore an expat especially if you're young and looking for adventure

- Not entirely quite especially during summertime because many people rent here during their summer vacations.

- There are lots of laws you need to abide when it comes to building your own house since it's a beachfront area. There are some laws that crushed an expats' dream of building their own beach houses.

- There aren't a lot of expats around during summertime because they only come here during winter or cold season
- Since this is a remote area, there aren't a lot of transportations around (unless you live in the center of Progresso area) so you might need a car, which of course, could be another expense.
- Tourists flock here once in a while because Progresso is a cruise ship destination
- Communication services may not be good

Holbox Island

- Such a beautiful and peaceful place
- Small island with limited neighborhoods and/or real estate
- Population here is only a few hundred people
- Doesn't have a lot of access to necessities

- Most expats who resides here are only temporary residents or business owners, and they don't stay very long since this is already a very remote place.
- Communication services is not good

Izamal

- A colonial village that is cozy and also peaceful
- It's about an hour away from the city of Merida
- Doesn't have a lot of access to necessities
- There are only a few expats in this area
- Ideal for artists, writers, and the likes that needed some sort of inspiration for creative purposes, or for people who needed some time to reflect.

Valladolid

- A colonial town that's about 2 hours away from the city of Merida
- Renting a place here is cheaper compared to other areas in Progresso
- Offers a peaceful living
- 2 hours away from Cancun Airport

- Doesn't have a lot of access to necessities like shopping places
- There are only a few expats in this area but the town is getting popular than ever so it might be an advantage for you
- The place is about to become fully developed (at the time of this writing).

Quintana Roo State

Another famous spot for expats is the Quintana Roo area. This is another large state with many districts and towns to choose from. The famous places where most foreigners reside include Cancun, Isla Mujeres, and Puerto Morelos, Talum, and Playa Del Carmen. Other expat states include Cozumel Island, Akumal, Puerto Adventuras, Paamul, Bacalar, and Mahahual (Costa Maya). It's a combination of international living and local living. The state is filled with expats and tourists but is not as intense as that of Merida.

If you wanted to enjoy the scenery, the beach, and the mixed cultures without too much of a hassle, then this place is for you. The European and western influences here abound, and you can also have access to not just basic necessities but also other international goodies. You will have a great time adjusting, and also have a chance to interact with not just expats but also tourists. This place will make you feel like home but in a much better setting.

Cancun

Cancun is the capital of the Quintana Roo state. It's a city famous for its white sandy beaches, and amazing hotels that attracts tourists all year round.

Advantages:

- Cancun is where the international airport is located. You'll have better access to flights from around the world at a much cheaper cost.
- The city was built in the 1970's which is why it's very modern
- Has many international establishments like malls, restaurants, condo units, entertainment places etc.
- You don't need to learn a lot of Spanish because since this is one of the leading tourist spots in Mexico, the main language here is English!
- There's a lot of beautiful beaches, nightclubs, and other trendy places
- Communication services is at its best

Disadvantages:

- You won't really feel like you're in Mexico because the city lacks a colonial and cultural ambiance to it.
- You would want to have a car because almost everyone here has a car.

- The city is mostly designed for tourists, so aside from beaches, cuisines, and high-rise malls there isn't much here you can explore.
- Not ideal for permanent residency because it's always crowded with tourists. Mainly ideal for young adventurers and/or temporary expats.

Isla Mujeres

This place is a tropical island, so if you dream of staying here to live the "carribean lifestyle." Then this is perfect for you!

Advantages:

- Since the island is long and narrow, you'll surely enjoy sightseeing or driving around town (using golf carts) to do your shopping.
- You'll have a spectacular view of the ocean right at your doorstep!
- An ideal place for retirees or those who loves the beach that aren't crowded with tourists

- Experiencing an ocean breeze, the sun at your face, and the fresh produce will now be a part of your life if you choose settles here.

Disadvantages:

- Isla Mujeres is considered a small an island (even if it's compared with island standards).
- Moving here can be a hassle especially if you have a family. You'll have to transport everything via ferry, and may need to constantly go to the city – center in Cancun if you need more than the basics.
- The ocean breeze can rapidly wear your house down so you might need to always maintain it.
- Communication services is not good
- Lots of tourists flock here during summer
- Life in an island might easily bore you if you are used to having a fast – paced lifestyle.

Puerto Morelos

This place is located at the south of the busy city of Cancun. It's another small fishing village that's also located in front of a beach. This is where an international show called House Hunters usually shoots their scenes for expats who are planning to move here.

Advantages:

- A place that has a small town feel, and is in close proximity to many beaches
- Very close to the city – center in Cancun which means you have full and easy access to malls, airports, dining places, and other entertainment spots
- A growing town with newly developed housing projects

Disadvantages:

- You would definitely need a car if you want to have access to the city life

- You can either stay in the ocean side of this town, while the other towns/areas are a bit far since Puerto Morelos is split in two.

- It's very expensive if you want to buy a beach front house because there are only limited houses. And since you're an expat, the owners might double the price on you compared to a local.

- The sea breeze can rapidly wear your house down so you might need to always maintain it (if you live in the sea side of town).

- Communication services may not be good

Playa Del Carmen

This is a city that is becoming more popular than ever. It's inhabited by nearly 200,000 residents and counting! Many expats and locals love here because it has a European ambiance mixed with South American culture that is also next to the ocean! There are a lot of housing styles, condos, and villas to choose from. You'll certainly have a lot of new foreign and local friends here as most expats already have their own communities that can surely help you adjust to your new life.

Advantages:

- According to most expats, Playa del Carmen is very different from most places in Mexico. It is unique because it's a combination of European and Latin cultures and influences.

- Everything is accessible and walking distance, and it also has a great transportation system

- There are a growing expat population making it very easy to meet with fellow foreigners and like-minded people.

- It's only 40 minutes away from the Cancun International Airport

- Since there are a lot of foreigners living here, the traditions are often celebrated especially in restaurants.

Disadvantages:

- There aren't much of a colonial culture and living surrounding it compared to states in the Yucatan area.

- Doesn't have a lot of shopping malls and big stores compared to Cancun

- Has limited beach front houses making buying a property there quite expensive

Cozumel Island

It is one of the most popular islands in Mexico, and it is inhabited by nearly 100,000 people. Most locals and expats live near the major town in the island so that basic needs can be access.

Advantages:

- Compared to other islands in Mexico, Cozumel Island has access to almost everything you'll need

- It's a great place for diving and snorkeling acitivities

- Cozumel Island belongs to the best places to relocate not just in Mexico but also in the world
- Ideal for retirees, young adventurers, and professional expats.
- Has its own international airport and ferry ports
- Only an hour away from Playa del Carmen

Disadvantages:

- Tourists flock here during summer, and cruise ports could be crowded during this time
- You might get easily bored because since this is an island there isn't much to do except for sightseeing and spending time at the beach.
- Communication may not be good
- Beach front houses could be expensive

Puerto Adventuras

This is quite an exclusive expat community surrounded by a marina. Most residents here get to enjoy driving around in golf carts to get from one place to another.

It's also inhabited by foreigners who have an upper class status.

Advantages:

- It's a safe and exclusive expat community
- You can have lots of housing styles and condos to choose from
- Filled with like – minded people

Disadvantages:

- Has one of the most expensive real estate options in Mexico
- Has lots of rules and regulations to abide
- Doesn't have a lot of access to shops, restaurants, and entertainment places
- A small and exclusive community that lacks cultural ambiance or a colonial feel to it.

Talum

This town is quite popular because of its Hispanic ruins. It also has an eco – friendly and quite trendy beach town that is slowly gaining popularity among expats and tourists alike.

Advantages:

- If you want to live in an eco – friendly type of environment with like – minded people, this is the place for you.
- There are lots of gourmet restaurants around as well as bakeries
- Has many beautiful beaches also attracts celebrities
- There's a lot of natural places to explore since the town is not yet fully developed.

Disadvantages:

- Real estate are already quite expensive because it's development is starting already

- Infrastructure and water supply are just being set up, there might be water interruptions among residents and rubbles along the way.

- There aren't many shopping places since it's a small town

- You might need a car because the transportation system is not yet that accessible.

Other Places in Quintana Roo for Expats

Akumal

- Famous for its beach turtles

- A coastal town that has high standard of living

- Has many luxurious condos and houses

- Not that accessible to malls

Paamul

- A seaside community

- Mostly a place for travellers and hikers

- Has a very cheap cost of living

- Close to many beaches but far from major necessities

Bacalar

- A small town that has a tropical setting
- Has its own lake
- Most expats who live here enjoys the remote living
- You may need to buy a car because it's far from major cities, airports, and shopping places.

Mahahual

- A small fishing village that has its own port
- A remote and coastal area
- Undeveloped, very peaceful, and has a Caribbean lifestyle
- Not ideal for permanent residency but if you like to have a small guest house then this is ideal

Cost of Living in Mexico

Depending on the city, state or town you choose to settle in, it's essential that you know how much your day to day expenses will be before you decide to move. Here's a breakdown of everything you might need when you relocate in Mexico. The currency is in Mexican dollars, so just convert these items in your national currency so you can have a gauge at the costs of each. This section will not cover every single thing, this is just to give you an idea of how much items could cost. Please also note that prices may vary at the time of the writing.

Food:	Average Cost (Mex Peso)
Lunch with drinks in Restaurants (business areas)	MXN140
Fast Food Combo Meal	MXN 90
1 litter of milk	MXN 17
2 eggs	MXN 30
1 kilogram of tomatoes	MXN 19
1 kilogram of potatoes	MXN 20
1 bottle of red wine	MXN 218
1 kilogram of apples	MXN 37

Clothes	Average Cost (Mex Peso)
1 pair of jeans (branded)	MXN 932
1 dress/ top dress (branded)	MXN 666
1 pair of rubber shoes (branded)	MXN 1,500
1 pair of leather shoes (branded)	MXN 1,600

Transportation/ Commute	Average Cost (Mex Peso)
Golf carts (for island living)	MXN 269, 899
1 liter of gas	MXN 17
Ticket for public transportation (taxis, buses, trains for 1 month)	MXN 500 more or less

Personal Care/ Utilities	Average Cost (Mex Peso)
1 month worth of electricity, gas, heaters etc.	MXN 1,700 more or less
1 month of Internet connection	MXN 368
TV (Flat Screen - 40")	MXN 8,450
Microwave	MXN 1,750
Cleaning help (per hour)	MXN 42
Antibiotics (1 box)	MXN 160
Generic Medicine (good for 6 days)	MXN 95 more or less
Deodorant (50 ml)	MXN 47

Shampoo (400 ml)	MXN 55
Toothpaste	MXN 30
Toilet Paper (4 rolls)	MXN 30
Medical Checkup (private doctor)	MXN 700 more or less (depends on how long/ conditions) etc.
Gym membership (1 month; business district)	MXN 1,250 more or less
Movie tickets (for 2)	MXN 160 more or less
1 beer (local pub)	MXN 50
Dinner for two in a fine dining (complete meal)	MXN 1,570

Chapter Four: Housing and Estate Planning

Now that you've learned the pros and cons of your possible living options, have seen the estimated costs of living, and already have an idea where most expats settle in Mexico, it's time to learn your best option in terms of housing and properties. This chapter will give you an overview of how an expat like you, whether you're planning to become a temporary or permanent resident, can acquire a house and/or properties in Mexico. It doesn't matter if you are a retiree, if you have a family, or you're a young blood looking for an awesome adventure, you'll need to ensure that you will be well – accommodated in the state you chose because after all, every home needs a house!

Renting vs. Buying

In this section, you'll see a new set of pros and cons if you were to rent a house/condo in Mexico or if you choose to buy a house/real estate. This is a great way for you to weigh your options before doing any investments.

You should make sure that whatever you do – whether you're renting or buying a place – should match your financial capacity and/or savings, should meet your purpose and standards, should enable you to access your basic necessities, and of course, make you feel truly at home. The last thing you want is to settle in an area you like but not stay in a house you feel comfortable living in. Sometimes expats, because of their excitement to buy a new house in a new country, find themselves unhappy after the fuzz is over because they made poor decisions and lacked proper planning.

Keep in mind that you're not just going to buy or rent a place, you're investing your hard – earned money! This is also where you'll be spending most of your time, so better be wise, and really weigh everything or consult the right people before investing or committing to this huge undertaking.

Here now are the pros and cons in renting and buying properties in Mexico:

Pros and Cons in Renting a House in Mexico

Pro#1: Renting keeps your options open.

As what you've seen from the previous chapter, there are lots of places in Mexico you can choose from. Your area of choice highly depends on your purpose, and the basic amenities you think that place can provide. However, as what the old adage says, *you'll never know unless you try.* You thought you want something but turns out you don't, renting will give you the option of quitting before committing!

The main advantage of renting a place is that you don't really need to commit yet to a certain neighborhood or house or whatnot. You can keep your options open before you finally decide what kind of place you would want to settle in for the long term.

Pro#2: Renting is flexible

In terms of financing your rent, this method gives you a very flexible option. You can rent for as short as a few weeks to a few months just to see what it will be like in that particular place or area, and you can also rent for the long term (5 years). You can also sublet your chosen apartment or house if say you're going away for an indefinite period of time. Win – win!

Pro#3: Renting only requires a minimum investment

Obviously, you do not need to go through the hassle of arranging real estate matters like property taxes, and won't need to pay a huge mortgage as compared to when you're buying your own property. You just need to pay a deposit for the first month of your stay (depends on the conditions of your landlord), and from there pay rent every month or whatever you and your landlord agreed to.

The rental prices on average costs around $350 to $1,200/ month depending on how large the house is, the location (obviously if the house is in a remote place or far from the city center, it'll be much cheaper – unless it's in front of a beach or around famous tourist spots), and the season (rental prices are at its peak around Nov – Apr; July – Aug).

Con#1: Housing arrangement/style/structure

Of course, you can't rent a place that you exactly like, and to your specifications. One way or another, there'll be something that you may not like in your chosen home but that's how it goes; you didn't build it in the first place. Most of the homes and apartments for rent are already fully furnished, the interior design may not be to your liking, and the choices could be limited depending on the area you want to be accommodated in.

Con#2: Landlords and Leaking Roofs

You might get to deal with Mexican landlords that are hard to talk to or come to an agreement to, which is why a rental contract or a written agreement is probably best so that you'll have something to show as proof that you agreed with the terms and conditions. According to most expats, the people managing the places are sometimes hard to talk to and even find! Make sure to get a receipt every time you pay your rent, and keep it.

When it comes to maintenance, make sure that the house is in good, if not best condition; otherwise you'll have difficulty managing it. It's also ideal that you talk to the previous renters if you can or the neighbors around just to learn a thing or two about what happened to the previous renter and why he/she moved out so that you'll have an idea of how the landlord manages the renters/house.

Pros and Cons in Buying a House in Mexico

Pro#1: Buying gives you complete control of everything

There are more houses in Mexico that are already built and available for purchase than a place for rent. You have complete control of what kind of house you want, the improvements and renovations you want to do, and have the freedom to choose the location you prefer. There will also be houses that will require a few structure investments before you can move in.

Pro#2: Buying a house in Mexico is quite easy.

If you don't want a lot of headaches, then make sure that you only buy from reputable real estate companies, and work with reputable lawyers. What you can do is to talk to fellow expats and even locals around the neighborhood so that you can get insights and recommendations.

You would want a so – called *Notario* at your corner when buying properties. Notarios in Mexico are government appointed lawyers and proprietors that handles property and housing transactions. They'll be able to help you in buying a property through a bank or acquire it through a Deed of Trust. If you work with the right people, buying a house will be easy.

Pro#3: Buying a house is an investment.

Some of you may not agree, but let's face it, buying a property is and can be considered an investment simply because it's something you own, and something that you can sell at a higher price than what you originally paid for. It's also a long – term investment that you can pass on to your children or heirs one day.

The economy in Mexico especially in terms of lands and properties has significantly increased over the last few years. The property taxes for foreigners are almost non – existent as well which means that you can sell your house without paying huge estate taxes as long as you've already owned the property for about 2 years already and have an FM3 or FM2 visa. You can flip houses you bought, and sell it at a better price especially if it's located in a great neighborhood.

The real estate or property taxes in Mexico costs only $72 in 1 year at the time of this writing – compared to say a real estate tax in California USA which is around $4,000/year.

Con#1: Buying a house needs a large initial investment

Most houses in Mexico are purchase with cash. Houses have an average cost of $30,000 to $1 million and above. Of course, it will depend on how large the property is, the amenities or furnishings included, the location, the quality or design of the construction, and other terms of payment. Most American and Canadian expats buys a house that costs around $60,000 to over $250,000. Make sure that before investing, you have the initial cash to pay upfront for the property, and you have enough cash to pay the lawyers/notaries you will hire, the processing fees, and real estate taxes/deeds.

Con#2: Buying a house lacks flexibility

Of course, compared to just renting a place, you can't just leave the property you bought if it turns out that you don't like the location of the area or you just don't feel like living in it anymore. And even if you sell your house, you need to ensure that you'll sell it at a higher price to recoup your investment in it – including the renovations you made, and the furnishings you bought as well as the other things that cost you. If you're always travelling, and leaving your house for long period of time, it might not be ideal because you might get robbed.

Con#3: Buying a house in Mexico requires extensive research

As an expat, it's your job to become an informed buyer so that you won't get scammed or you don't settle for something that you have no idea about. Ensure that you have the full picture especially when it comes to agreements, laws, taxes, and everything. There are only few consumer protection laws in Mexico and there are also no mandatory inspections so be careful, learn as much as you can before signing anything, and get recommendations from fellow expats.

Questions to Ask when Renting a House

Aside from the basic renting questions, here are some things you should ask your landlord before renting a place out in Mexico:

- Is the electricity, water, and gas already arranged or hooked up in the house or do I need to arrange it myself?

- How's the water situation? Is there a water purifier? Does it require maintenance? Do I need to change the filter?

- Is the communication services like phones, and internet included in the house rent or do I need to arrange this separately?

- What were the previous maintenance problems (if any)? Can you recommend someone who knows how to fix stuff if ever? If the house has a garden, ensure that you ask your landlord if he/she can recommend a gardener, and if it's already included in the house rental payment (homes with gardens usually includes a gardener already). The same goes if you rented a house with a swimming pool.

- Is there a fire alarm in cases of emergencies? Is there a water pump etc.? How does it work?

Questions to Ask when Buying House/Property

Here are some of the questions you need to consider before you buy a property in Mexico:

- How big of house do you need? One bedroom, two?
- What will be its purpose? Is it only a guest house for you? Will you live here? Will you have people come here all the time?

- What kind of style do you like? An apartment? A two – storey house etc.?

- Do you prefer to have a garden? A pool? A backyard?

- Can you maintain the house and afford the maintenance costs in the future?

- What location do you prefer? Do you want to live in the city – center, in a remote place, in a village, in a beach front?

- Do you want to live in an exclusive expat community? Or do you want to live among the locals?

- Is your home near landmarks, and important establishment? Is it located in a place where you have an easy access to transportation and basic necessities? Needless to say, is it convenient?

- Do you prefer a fully furnished home? Most houses for sale in Mexico doesn't come with furniture so you'll have to purchase for yourself and take care of all the household needs.

- What's your budget? Make sure that you know your price limitation including everything that you need to pay for including the services, taxes, maintenance, etc.

Frequently Asked Questions about Expats or Foreigners

Owning a Property in Mexico

Can a foreigner own a property in Mexico?

Yes! Expats can buy a house or a house and lot in the country including properties that are located in border and coastal areas. You also don't need to be a permanent resident holder to buy a property. Most expats buy lands in any state/ areas (including beach fronts and islands) through placing the property in a bank trust.

Who are the people/professionals that I need to talk to if I place my property through a bank trust?

You'll encounter the seller otherwise known as the Trustor, and the Fiduciario/ Trustee (bank). You, the buyer, will be called as the beneficiary or Fideicomisario.

What are the charges and how much are the fees in a bank trust?

As the time of this of writing, the initial fee you need to pay is US$500 in order to establish the trust fund. The bank will also collect an annual fee upfront of around US $500 (fees are subject to change depending on the banks). You might also need to pay other additional charges for services which could cost another US $500 to US $600 on average.

How does the bank trust work?

The property's title is will be transferred to the bank since the bank is the Trustee. The Trust Agreement will then be subject for approval by the Mexico's Ministry of Foreign Affairs. Once the permit is issued, you as the buyer/beneficiary will have rights to the property and will also be recorded in the Public Notary of Mexico.

What are my rights as a beneficiary?

You have the right to sell your property to anyone or transfer the title to your chosen heir. The Trustee (bank) will still be the legal holder of the property.

Who are the professionals involved when buying real estate?

The people involved includes the real estate company, the seller/agent, the bank, Public Notary/ lawyer/s, and you, the buyer.

What is the function of a Public Notary?

Public Notaries or the so – called Notarios in Mexico are lawyers appointed by the government that handles property transactions, process, approves and certifies all the official documents related to real estate ownership to ensure that the property is transferred smoothly to the rightful owner.

What official documents?

Real estate documents required by Mexican law include a no-lien certificate based on a complete title search from the Public Property Registry, municipality statements of property assessments, taxes, appraisal etc.

Who will pay the closing costs if I decided to buy or sell a property? And how much does it costs?

The buyer usually pays for the closing costs including acquisition taxes, transfer taxes, Public Notary fees, bank charges, and the likes. The total closing costs usually is around 3% to 5% of the selling price.

How much do I need to pay for the transfer tax?

Transfer tax is around 2% to 4% of the tax appraisal value

How long will this whole process take before I can acquire my desired property?

It usually takes 1 to 2 months, since you're a foreigner and you're only way of acquisition is through a Bank Trust.

Mexicans only takes about a week to buy a property and get it processed.

Where and how should I pay for the property?

You'll need to pay it through a third party escrow service. They manages the transaction for the buyer and seller.

Why is it better to buy a property from a realtor than an agent?

This is because realtors are considered as professional real estate agents that are members of the National Association of Realtors and the Mexican Association of Professional Real Estate Agents (AMPI). They are certified agents, and they follow strict codes of conduct and adhere to rules. Make sure to buy from an AMPI real estate agent.

Estate Planning

The main function of estate plans is to properly and smoothly distribute your property or properties whether it is a land, and/or a house and lot to your children or chosen heirs when you pass away. Many people or families are familiar with their estate plans but most people are not, and this is why problems arise. Many only availed a one – size – fits – all plan, and not even bothered in seeking any legal professional to customize their chosen plans in order to meet their needs and/or wishes.

Estate planning involves making a written will. A will that is properly signed and witnessed is very important because it gives the piece of paper the power to legally pass the property or titles to the rightful heirs once the owner dies. If you're an expat or someone who bought a house or property in Mexico, it's highly recommended that you create a written will to ensure that the properties you bought and worked hard for will go to the right person/s, and will go through an easy legal process. Here are the benefits of having a will:

- A will establishes how you want your lands or properties to be given away.

- A will entitles you're young children to the properties you own, and you have the power to choose or appoint the guardian, until your children is of the right age to claim it.
- A will gives clear instructions on how your properties or assets will be disposed and enables you/your heirs to also lower or not pay for any probate expenses.

- A will avoids disputes between family members.

- A will is not that expensive to arrange, and won't take too much of your time during preparation. Drafting a will in Mexico only costs US$250.

- A will prevents the judge to decide on who, where, and how your properties will be given away. If you own properties, and have not written any will in Mexico or even in other countries, the judge will be forced to act upon the law and take things in their own hands. Having a written will enables you to decide these private matters, and will also be less of hassle for your family that will be left behind.

Here are the disadvantages of not having a written will for your assets in Mexico:

- In Mexico, if you passed away without having written a will, and only survived by your spouse, your estate will be equally divided among your spouse, AND your parents.

- If it's survived by your spouse and children, usually the law requires that the estate shall be divided equally between the spouse and the children. But, if the spouse has its own assets/properties that will exceed or is equal to the portion given to the children, the surviving spouse will not or may not inherit the property/assets of the deceased.

- Not having a written will can be much more complicated if the deceased has children from prior marriages or from third parties. The heirs usually don't agree when it comes to how much should be disposed for each of them. This leads to terrible family disputes.

- If you don't have a written will, as mentioned earlier, the properties will be subject to a court process called Probate. This is where the judge will decide on how the property/estates/assets should be dispose. The probate process in Mexico is usually carried out by a Notario (laywers), and is done in a private affair unless there is a court challenge or if the heirs are underage. When this happens, the probate process will involve courts. The good thing is that this probate process only takes about 3 to 6 months in Mexico.

- If you're a foreigner and also have properties in other countries then it's highly recommended that you create wills for each country. This is advantageous because each wills will be handled by an executor from where the will is drafted. If the properties you have in Mexico have its own will, then a Mexican executor will take care of it, and prevents revoking any other wills you may have.

Wills are perhaps the most important document you will ever sign in your life especially if you have a family. It will also guarantee you that your wishes will be granted and respected once you pass. It will also save you and your family lots of time, lots of expenses, and lots of possible heartaches.

Other Estate Planning Tools

Aside from wills, there are other tools you can use when planning for your estate. These can all be in conjunction with your written will to ensure that all your properties and assets will be transferred to your heirs properly, and in the best possible way. If you want to learn more about them, and how it works in Mexico, it's best for you to do your own research, and talk to legal professionals so they can advise you as to the best option to take because these matters will vary depending on your situation, and/or needs. Other estate planning tools include the following:

- Trusts
- Prenuptial Agreement
- Living Will
- Life Insurance
- Business succession plan
- Healthcare
- Power of Attorney

Chapter Five: Utilities and Communication Services in Mexico

Once you've taken care of knowing where you want to live, have considered your living options, and you're now preparing to acquire a certain property, it's time to learn a thing or two about the utilities you'll need, and the communication services being offered in Mexico. This is all essential especially for expats like you who are either moving there to work or to study. Knowing your options particularly for mobile and internet connections will enable you to see what will fit your budget, what will be best for your needs, and what kind of service you can expect. We will provide a breakdown of all the possible options in this chapter to give you an idea.

Utilities in Mexico

Electricity in Mexico

The electricity in Mexico is much cheaper and affordable compare to other countries. Foreign nationals can also take advantage of the higher currency rates of their national money once it is exchange in Mexican currency. Of course, this highly depends on how much you consume per kilowatt. However, in Mexico it can all change depending on what state or city you are residing and even the neighborhood of your choice.

You'll most probably pay approximately $10 - $50 per electric bill if you are residing in an average sized city or if you are in neighborhoods that have lower to middle class income. If you chose to live in luxurious villas or exclusive villages, your electric bill may cost around $200 and up. The coverage of electricity in Mexico is billed every 2 months.

Water in Mexico

Water bills are just the same with electric bills; it is billed every 2 months, and the cost depends on your residential area. The price ranges from as little as $5 to $50 and more. What you should do before buying or renting a house in Mexico is to ask the owner if you can see the previous bills so that you'll have an idea at how much it would cost on average as well as the average consumption. It's also ideal to ask around your neighbors regarding the quality of service for both water and electricity before you buy or rent a property in a particular area you prefer.

You want to make sure that the supply of electricity and water is great, that the quality is great, and the service is also at its best so that you'll know if the provider is reliable in cases problems arise. You should also try to ask what happens during instances where electricity and water supply is cut – off for various reasons, and what are the alternative options.

As mentioned earlier, you should also ask the owner if the electricity and water supplies are already connected in the house because if not, it's up to you on how you're going to set up your electric and water connection by either calling your preferred service provider or asking help from your landlord to hook up your connections.

Payment Options

Payment for both electric and water bills can be done in local banks, selected grocery stores and convenience stores or directly from the electric and water companies. Sometimes the companies provide their own centers or booths near major outlets so you can easily pay your bills. You could also try their online payment options if it's available so that you won't need to go out every time you pay. Do take note that charges and hidden fees may apply so make sure to ask your service provider about these details.

Gas in Mexico

Another major utility you need to set up before moving in is gas. In Mexico, you can buy a gas directly from the company/businesses. It is either delivered to you once you order a tank or like what most locals do, they wait for trucks that carry gases in the streets if they want to order. You'll certainly hear these trucks once they roam around your neighborhood because they have what Mexicans call "gas bells" like a fire alarm alerting you that they're delivering gas. These trucks pass by almost every day around certain areas.

If you're in far flung places, you might need to call up your gas provider so that they can deliver a tank at your house. However, delivery charges may apply. A small tank can last for 1 to 2 months depending on your consumption. The price of gas in Mexico is constantly changing because it is set by the government just like in other countries.

Mobile Plans in Mexico (for Expats from the U.S. and Canada)

This section will focus on the plans you can avail if you're an expatriate from America and Canada. Since these countries are in close proximity to one another, lots of mobile companies in the U.S. are now offering lots of deals and package plans for international clients especially for expats who are now residing in Mexico and for travellers as well. Most of these plans will enable you to call to and from Mexico, to and from the United States, and to and from Canada for a relatively cheaper amount. It also comes with lots of different features and services.

We've compiled the leading international mobile providers in the table below. This is also an advantage for you to compare prices, features, and package deals so that you'll know what best suits you and your needs.

Provider: T – Mobile

General Features:

- Unlimited Calls to and from Mexico and Canada
- Unlimited Texts to and from Mexico and Canada
- Data allowance without roaming frees to and from Mexico
- Has other features including unlimited music streaming
- Unlimited international texting to over 140 countries
- Unlimited 2G/3G data

Mobile Plans:

Simply Prepaid Plan 10 GB

Price: US$50

Features:

- Has 10GB LTE Data
- Unlimited Data, National Talk & Text
- 1 month prepaid
- Comes with free prepaid sim (for in – store purchases only)

One (Unlimited 55+) Plan

Price: US$50/month (with US$25 upfront payment)

Features:

- Unlimited Data, National Talk & Text

- No contract

- Included for One Plus and One Plus International Plan holder

Simply Prepaid Plan 6 GB

Price: US$55

Features:

- Has 6GB LTE Data

- Unlimited Data, National Talk & Text

- 1 month prepaid

- Comes with free prepaid sim (for in – store purchases only)

Provider: Cricket

General Features:

- Unlimited Calls between Mexico, US, and Canada (no roaming fees)
- Unlimited Texts between Mexico Mexico, US, and Canada (no roaming fees)
- Data allowance without roaming frees in Mexico and Canada
- Unlimited domestic texts, and texts from the U.S. to over 38 countries
- You can save $5 every month if you pay using AutoPay.

Unlimited Plan with AutoPay

Price: US$50/month (with $9.99 upfront payment)

Features:

- Unlimited Data, National Talk & Text
- No Contract

Provider: Sprint

General Features:

- Unlimited texts in Canada, Mexico and to over 160 countries
- Unlimited 2G roaming data in Canada, Mexico and to over 160 countries
- 4G LTE data roaming for $2/day or $10/week both in Mexico and Canada

Forward Single Line Plan

Price: US$40

Features:

- 4 GB Data
- Unlimited Data, National Talk & Text
- No Contract
- 1 month prepaid

Single Line 2GB Plan

Price: US$40/month

Features:

- 2 GB Data

- Unlimited Data, National Talk & Text

- No Contract

- Comes with free activation for all devices

Provider: AT & T

General Features:

- Unlimited texts and calls free of roaming charges in Mexico and Canada

- Unlimited calls and roaming from the US to Mexico and also in Canada

AT & T Prepaid $30 Monthly Plan

Price: US$30/month (with $9.99 upfront payment)

Features:

- 1 GB Data

- Unlimited Data, National Talk & Text

- 1 month prepaid

AT & T Prepaid $40 Monthly Plan

Price: US$40/month (with $9.99 upfront payment)

Features:

- 6 GB Data
- Unlimited Data, National Talk & Text
- 1 month prepaid

Provider: Verizon Wireless

General Features:

- Unlimited Calls with free roaming in Mexico and Canada with Verizon Unlimited plans
- You can have the option to add $15/ $25 in your Mexico or Canada plan
- If you're not in an unlimited plan, you can still use the existing data, calls, and text on your plan allowance with an additional of $5/day.

Verizon Wireless Prepaid $40 Prepaid Plan

Price: US$40

Features:

- 3 GB Data
- Unlimited Data, National Talk & Text
- 1 month prepaid

Verizon Wireless Prepaid $50 Prepaid Plan

Price: US$40

Features:

- 7 GB Data

- Unlimited Data, National Talk & Text

- 1 month prepaid

Internet Access in Mexico

Although there are many internet providers in Mexico, the main ISP provider and leading Telecom Company is the Telmex Network. They often bundle their services including the telephone connection, internet, and cable so that locals and foreigners alike can avail all their services at a discounted price.

Under the Telmex (Telefonos de Mexico) network is called Prodigy Internet. It currently holds 92% of the market shares in Mexico when it comes to providing internet. It's also the leading company providing Wi-Fi and DSL broadband access. Another popular provider in Mexico is called Terra. Hot spots/Wi - Fi for you to have access to the internet on the go are also operated by Telmex under

Prodigy Moyil. It's available in Mexico especially in city –

centers, malls, selected groceries, restaurants, coffee shops,

and other major outlets/ establishments. If you don't have a

plan under the Telmex company or Prodigy Internet, you'll

need to buy a sim card called Tarjeta Multifon before you

can connect to the Wi – Fi. It's available in many gadget

stores and convenient stores as well.

Here are the features of the Prodigy Infinitum Plan

for your internet connection:

Provider: Telmex Network

Plan: Prodigy Infinitum Plan

- Comes in 512kbits/s, 1024 kbit/s, 2048 kbit/s, and 4096

  kbit/s internet speed.

- The cheapest plan cost US$30/ month compared to the

  cheapest internet plan of Verizon Wireless in the US

  which is only $14.99/month.

- Installation and the modem are free of charge.

- No need to sign a service contract

- Once you subscribed, it allows you to have free access to public Wi – Fi hotspots since Prodigy is also the main service provider.

Provider: GLOBALSAT

- This is another internet provider for residents in Mexico especially those living in remote areas.

- The internet services and plans are very expensive

- Installation may not be free, and you may need to provide your own internet equipment which will require initial investment on your part.

- GLOBALSAT boasts complete coverage in all of Mexico even in places where telephone lines are not available or places that are out of coverage.

Chapter Six: Work and Business in Mexico

This chapter is for expats who are planning to reside in Mexico for work or business purposes. The information that will be provided here could also help foreigners who are planning to be temporary residents, and may think about getting a job while staying in Mexico for a period of time We will cover the basic topics on how to apply for work in Mexico, the kinds of jobs a foreigner can apply to, the permits you'll need, and the basic minimum wage.

This chapter will also cover how an expat like you can set up your own business, the permits you need to have, and the process of registering your business. This will all be essential to ensure that you won't break any laws regarding earning money and making a living in Mexico.

Working in Mexico

First and foremost, foreigners can definitely work in Mexico as long as you have the right permit/s, and if you meet the criteria. Check out the following rules below to see if you are eligible to work in Mexico:

- If you are a foreigner that is sponsored or hired by a Mexican company, **or**
- If you are a foreigner that is sponsored or hired by a foreign/ international company with a Mexican subsidiary or operations, **or**
- If you are a foreigner that has specific skills needed and/or required in Mexico, **or**
- If you are a foreigner that is sponsored or hired by a foreign company as long as you do not receive any

payment directly from a Mexican company and/or its subsidiaries.

Common Jobs of Foreigners in Mexico

Here are some of the most common jobs that foreign nationals and expats have during their stay in Mexico:

- **Corporate Employee**

  Foreigners usually move to Mexico because their company reassigned them to do their job in a company or manufacturing facilities that are located here. This usually happens especially to foreign employees of huge multi – national companies. These employees are reassigned for a period of time in order to carry out their duties and also handle or report to the management. This is also the most common route of foreigners especially if they wanted to apply for a temporary or even permanent residency in the country. The main advantage of being reassigned is that most companies will sponsor you and will take care of all the legalities, expenses, logistics, and visa needed in order for you to legally work in Mexico.

- **Self - Employment**

  Some foreigners are also self – employed which means they either set up a small business in the country like a consulting service, a restaurant, bars etc. They also get to earn money by providing a specialized service using their skills in computer, business development, architecture, and other related fields through getting their own local clients.

- **English Teachers**

  Some foreigners are hired in Mexico to teach the English language. In fact, it's one of the most popular jobs an expat can take in Mexico. However, if you wish to apply for these kinds of jobs, you'll most likely need to be certified. A common certificate required is called a TEFL certificate. The requirements/ certifications/ trainings needed before you can teach English will vary depending on what the private schools or language centers in Mexico requires. The demand is quite high because learning the English language is a huge part of the academic curriculum in Mexico.

- **Social Work/ Religious Work**

  Some expats come to Mexico because they want to do various social projects, community service and/or religious work. Through these kinds of jobs, they are able to impart their knowledge and experiences to the locals. They also get to gain amazing experiences and learn the Mexican culture and way of life. However, this kinds of work is usually sponsored by foundations, religious organizations, or a non – government organization (NGO), and social workers are usually unpaid so this is like a volunteer kind of work, though some organizations may give an allowance. Foreigners don't need a work permit if they are under these circumstances, and they can stay at a maximum of 6 months in Mexico.

- **Casual/ Freelance/ Part – Time Jobs**

   Some foreigners or expats are seeking freelance works or part – time jobs which is usually illegal or let's just say 'under the radar.' However, it is becoming increasingly difficult to find such jobs or even set up small stores in flea markets because the Mexican immigration is strict when it comes to expats or foreigners operating casual businesses since these types of businesses are not properly registered. You can of course accept freelance jobs/ part – time jobs without needing paperwork but often times, these jobs are poorly paid, and is only treated as a sideline.

FAQs about Working in Mexico

Should I be living in Mexico for me to work there?
Not really but of course this will depend on your work situation and requirements. If you're only going to work in Mexico, and the job will only take a few days or a few months (not exceeding 6 months), then you may not need to get a work permit or additional paperwork. If this is the case, the law under the business section of the tourist visa

will apply. Consult the immigration office for further details. If your job will take more than 6 months to a year or so, then you'll definitely need a working permit or apply for a temporary resident visa for you to legally stay in the country.

What kind of permits do I need so that I can work in Mexico legally?

There are different kinds of work permits that are available; this of course will depend on your work requirements, your purpose, and how long you need to stay in the country.

How much is the minimum wage in Mexico?

This will highly depend on your position, and the company you'll work for. The minimum wage for an employee is around Mex$70 - $73 (or USD$4 – $4.25)

Doing Business in Mexico

If you are thinking of setting up a (small to medium sized) business in Mexico, you'll need to consider the federal, municipal, and state regulations where you'll want to build or set up your business/ company. You'll usually need to also deal with permits, register properties (if any), set up contracts, and the likes.

The people/ regulatory bodies that you'll need to deal with when you decide to set up your business in Mexico are the following:

- Notario Publico (public lawyers)
- Mexican Tax Authorities

- Registry for Foreign Investments (if you or your business partners don't have any permanent resident visas or are not planning to have one).

The process for registering businesses in Mexico won't take a long time (though it may vary) but it's not that difficult as long as you follow the rules, submit the right requirements, and pay the needed fees. The requirement for registrations and licenses also vary depending on the nature of the business you will establish, the business sector it will belong to, and the states and municipalities where it is established. It's highly recommended that you sought professional or legal advice so that you'll know the best option to take and because it can save you lots of time and energy.

FAQs about Setting Up a Business in Mexico

Who can establish a business in Mexico?

You can set-up or open a business in Mexico if:

- You have the legal right to be in the country

- You appointed a power of attorney as part of the startup process of the business

The Mexican government does not distinguish a foreign or domestic business ownership but if a company is owned/partly – owned by a foreigner who does not have permanent residency in the country, he/she should declare it to the Ministry of Foreign Investments.

Which states do foreigners or expats usually set up their businesses?

According to a recent survey by DoingBusiness.org, the most common places/states in Mexico where foreigners establish their small to medium size businesses or even companies is in Colima, Merida, Celaya, Aguascalientes, and Guadalajara.

Most Common Types of Business Entities in Mexico

This section will give you an overview of the common types of business entities that are usually formed in Mexico. It's actually similar to most countries. Take note of the following so that you'll know what will best suit you and your business:

- **Sociedad Anónima** (Public Limited Company/ Corporation)

  The Sociedad Anónima either has a variable or fixed capital. If the company has a variable capital, it will be referred to or classified as Sociedad Anónima de Capital Variable. The minimum capital is also fixed by the law but it doesn't necessarily mean that the capital should be paid during incorporation.

- **Sociedad de Responsabilidad Limitadada** (LLC/ Limited Liability Company)

  This kind of entity also has either a fixed or variable capital, but the name of the company will be the same, whether it has a fixed or variable company.

- **Sole Trader** (Sole Proprietor)

  This is for an individual who doesn't have any business partners, and would want to set up a business activity of their own using their own name for business and also tax purposes. They will be classified as Persona Física con actividad empresarial by Mexican Tax authorities.

- **Sociedad Civil** (similar to freelance businesses)
  This type of business is best suited for people who are providing professional services, and does not deal with any form of products or tangible goods. Examples of these individuals are doctors, consultants, accountants etc.

- **Asociacion Civil** (non – profit organizations)
  This is used for foundations, charities, and other non – profit organization such as clubs, trade associations, cooperatives etc.

How to Set Up/ Register a Business in Mexico

This section will give you a quick run – down of the process in registering a business in Mexico (with the exception of a sole proprietor):

Step #1: Register your company name

You have to ensure that your business or company name is available and is not identical with any other existing businesses. You should register it at the Secretaria de Economia (Departmen for Trade in Mexico); this can be done online at <www.tuempresa.gob.mx> or through a Notary Public. You might also need to pay up a registration fee to reserve the name of your company.

Step #2: Draft the Deed of Incorporation

After registering your company name, the next step is to set up a meeting or appointment with your lawyer or with a Notary Public in Mexico to create a draft of the Deed of Incorporation. This is a document stating who will be involved or regarded as partners in the business/corporation, as well as their rights, functions, positions, and the specific shares for each owner of the company.

Step #3: Sign the Deed of Incorporation to make it official

When everything is drafted already, the next thing you and/or your business partners should do is to sign the document. You'll need to sign it with the presence of a Notary Public/lawyer to have a legal effect. The presence of all the owners or business partners/associates that are mentioned in the Deed of Incorporation is a must. Another requirement is the identification documents of each owner. If the owner/s are foreigners, you'll need to present a passport, proof of legal presence like a working permit, tourist visas, and temporary or permanent resident visas. As well as the proof of address of each founder/owner, an example is a recent utility bill.

Step #4: Registration of Business Address

You should register the business address of your company as well.

Step #5: Registration of Business Tax

You should also register/file the taxes of the company at the Mexican Tax Authorities, which can be done at any local offices near your establishment.

Step #6: Notify the Local Government upon opening of your business/company

It is quite necessary to notify the local government where your business is established in once you open it to the public.

Step #7: Register your employees

Make sure all the employees that you'll hire at the Mexican Social Security Institute as well as the National Worker's Housing Fund. This is the right of every employee.

Step #8: Register your business/company to the Foreign Investment Register and the SIEM.

You should also register your company at the National Business Information Registry or SIEM as well as the Foreign

Investment Register especially if the owner/s do not have a

permanent residency status.

Chapter Seven: Family & Education in Mexico

Mexico is one of the top countries that are best for families because it has a great sense of a work – life balance. Foreigners, particularly Americans and Canadians chose to reside here with their children and relatives because it's also in close proximity to their home countries. It's advantageous on their part since they can easily go back to their hometowns anytime they want, and they also get to immerse themselves in a culture that is quite new but somewhat familiar.

One of the major reason why expats love staying or residing in Mexico is because of its very welcoming and hospitable environment. There are already a lot of expat communities all over Mexico that has been established which makes adjusting to a new life easier, familiar, and more fun.

Aside from the favorable exchange rate, and many housing/living options, there are also lots of working opportunities that awaits any expat especially those who are looking to take their careers/businesses to the next level or new directions, making it a perfect place for foreigners with families and children. Residing in Mexico can definitely impact a kid's cultural and social perspective. They'll get to be immersed in a new way of life, get to interact with other locals, and also have a different worldview.

The school system in Mexico is also fantastic! There are a lot of schools, both private and public as well as tertiary/ universities, that you can enroll your children into. You can also have the option of homeschooling your kids or enrolling them in International schools where most of the expats' children also study. This chapter will give you an overview of what it will be like for you and your family once you moved to this amazing place filled with the most hospitable people you've even seen.

Living in Mexico as an Expat Family

There are many things to consider and factors to weigh in if you're planning to move to Mexico with your whole family. Aside from finding the best school for your kids, you also need to factor in your daily financial and logistical needs as well as family – friendly services, not to mention, the healthcare and safety concerns for your family.

According to a recent national survey, Mexico is included as one of the top 20 countries (and the only one in Latin America) that expats choose to move into with their families. That's great news if you're planning to move here with your wife and kids for good because you know you're in good company. Mexico's very friendly and welcoming attitude as well as its vibrant cultural environment makes it the best choice for expat families as their new home.

This section will focus on some important factors on why Mexico is one of the top residential choices of expat families. Whatever kind of living environment you choose, the pace of life you want to experience, the cuisines you wanted to taste, the kind of education you want your children to have, and the comfortable life you dream of having, there's always something for everyone in this great country of Mexico.

Mexico Provides Urban Comfort

As mentioned in previous chapters, there are lots of living options in Mexico. If you and you're family wanted to move in a place that is somewhat familiar or similar to your urban lifestyle back home, then you can choose to buy or rent a house in many amazing cities of Mexico. Most expat families especially those who are working or running a business in the country is choosing to stay in Mexico's major metropolitan areas or urban cities including Guadalajara, Acapulco, Mexico City, and Monterrey.

This is mainly because everything that you'll need is already there – the shopping places, schools, religious places, landmarks, entertainment places, and various modern amenities. The transportation systems are also very accessible making it a convenient choice if you and you're family loves to go out and travel. The pace of life (although quite slower than most countries like USA), and the large community of expats from all over the world also adds to the beauty of living in major cities and urban areas in Mexico.

Most families also move to the metropolis because since these places are more expat – centric than those of rural or remote areas, lots of people here, including the locals, can speak and understand English. However, the main disadvantage is that such places could also have a higher cost of living especially when it comes to the prices of properties, food, utility bills, and other services you and your family need for your day to day living.

This is also one of the reasons why a lot of expat families decide to stay in a place outside of the city or even in quite remote places (either near coastal areas or small villages) because the cost of living there is much cheaper compared to living in an urban area. However, the common downside is accessibility and convenience but some people like to reside in these places because it's also away from the hustle and bustle of the city, and because they get to immerse themselves more in the Mexican culture compared to major cities.

Mexico is a top tourist destination

We all know that Mexico has a lot of great landmarks, beaches, and amazing sceneries. This is why a lot of expat families also like to move here. In fact, most of them have already spent some time travelling to and from Mexico before they decided to reside here for good or at least for a temporary period. The country is filled with many amazing and fun tourist spots that are family – friendly, and also budget – friendly making it a great choice for anyone looking to work, raise a family, and also have a great time.

Some expats who are working in remote places or beach locations like Cancun, Rivera Maya, and Puerto Vallarta are fortunate enough to really do some work, have access to top tourist spots, and do many leisure activities. However, if you and you're family decided to reside near tourist destinations, the cost of living might also be quite expensive since this is a tourist hub.

Mexico offers a cultural way of living

Most expat families wanted to move here because they are looking to immerse themselves and their children to a different and foreign culture. This is the reason why some families choose to stay in small towns instead of urban areas because aside from the fact that it's more affordable, expat parents like to expose their children to a different form of lifestyle. The only downside is that many modern amenities may not be available, and since these are far flung places, access to things like a high – speed internet connection, transportation system and the likes may be limited. The upside though is that you and your children will have an authentic cultural experience, and become one of them Mexicans – and that is priceless.

Important Things to Consider Before Moving Your Family in Mexico

Mexico is undoubtedly a great place to relocate with your family, but before deciding to move here, you should also make sure that you and your spouse have considered other important factors like safety, education and language, healthcare, and also immigration. You have to weigh the pros and cons, the possible consequences and rewards, and do full assessments of your family situation before you make any decisions.

This section will give you an overview of some important factors that you need to take into consideration so that you'll know if Mexico is the right country for you and your loved ones.

Safety and Security

One of the most important things you need to consider especially if you have young children is if the country you're going to move in is a safe and secure place. All countries have its good and dark side so to speak, and as you may know, Mexico is not an exemption. Mexico definitely have had its fair share of major headlines in the news - from simple disputes among its citizens resulting in crimes to drug cartel issues and the like.

There are areas in Mexico where criminal activity is very evident, so you might want to stay away from those places. This is why research, interviews, and even a quick visit is important because it will give you an idea of what is the living situation like in a particular area or neighborhood. This will also give you an idea if this is the kind of place you want to raise your family in. The good news is that the majority of the country is safe for expats and local citizens alike, and it's unaffected by serious issues facing the country.

Language and Education Systems

Even if there are a lot of Mexicans who know how to speak in English and can understand this language, Spanish is still the native tongue. If you enroll your kids in school (especially a public school), they may have a hard time coping up if they don't understand Spanish – which is why taking short courses or teaching them the basics is very ideal so that they won't be totally clueless. Learning Spanish, as mentioned in previous chapters, is also essential to your day to day life.

For families with school – age children, you'll need to weigh your options when picking the right institution to enroll your kids into so that they may gain proper education abroad. You might be wondering what the educational system is like in Mexico, while most schools here have a great educational system; there are still lots of improvement needed. Some schools in the country particularly those public schools in rural areas are quite behind compared to the rest of the country. According to recent survey, the educational system in most public schools is below average particularly in major subjects like science, mathematics, and reading – comprehension.

This is the reason why alternative learning systems like homeschooling, and international schools became popular because it can provide possibly a better educational option for your children.

Changes in Immigration

Changes in immigration are one of the most important things to consider before you move to Mexico. The changes in government and immigration laws can certainly affect you as expats. There could be growing uncertainties as to how such changes can affect foreigners planning to work or reside in Mexico, so just make sure that you're always updated, and informed about the recent changes before you make your move.

Healthcare

Expats particularly those with families may not be able to get a healthcare coverage yet especially if you do not hold a temporary or permanent resident status. You have to inquire if your healthcare provider in your home country will cover you if in case anything happens to you and your family while in Mexico. Otherwise, it's probably best that you either avail a medical coverage in Mexico (if you can) or from an international healthcare provider. Be sure to also have a budget for emergency situations for the whole family so that you'll be prepared financially if anyone gets sick.

School Options and Education Systems in Mexico

As mentioned earlier, the public school system in Mexico is quite behind in terms of education, and that's because of varied reasons. There's also a huge percentage of Mexicans dropping out in school because most children particularly those in high school and college needs to already start working so that they can help their families. On the other hand, schools in rural areas are usually underfunded by the government which is why the education system is not at its best. Shortage of teachers, lack of school facilities, textbooks, school supplies, and the likes are the usual reasons why public school systems don't have high standards.

The best schools to enroll your children is in private schools (mostly located in urban areas), and international schools because these schools have a bilingual form of education that can be best suited for expats.

The basic education in Mexico has 3 levels; primary school (from Grades 1 to 6) also known as *Primaria*, Junior High (from Grades 7 to 9) or *Secundaria*, and Senior High (from Grades 10 to 12) known in Mexico *Preparatoria*, and of course, tertiary level or college.

Some expat parents, particularly those who homeschool their kids, send their children to a Mexican school in the morning, and homeschool them in the afternoon. The reason is so that the kids will learn how to speak Spanish as well as get fully immersed and acclimated in the Mexican culture.

Types of Schools in Mexico

There are four types of school in Mexico, these are the following:

- Public Schools
- Private Schools (Bilingual/Bicultural)
- International Schools
- Universities/Colleges

There are lots of school options if you live in larger states or cities, but perhaps the main factors you need to consider is the academic standard of the school, traffic, travel time, and the tuition fees as these can be limiting factors when deciding what's best for your kids. Most expats with families choose to reside in an area where the school is accessible (even without a car), and near their homes.

There are also limited bilingual/bicultural schools; most of these schools are abundant in urban areas or major cities only. These schools offer foreign types of educational systems mixed with local education. For (temporary) expats who wish to continue their studies in Mexico, they can also enroll in an International Baccalaureate course but only some schools offer it, mostly private and international schools only or in a recognized Mexican university.

Public Schools

- Usually free of charge (but only for Mexican nationals, foreign expats might have miscellaneous fees)
- Secular (religious instructions are banned in public schools)
- The government also provides free textbooks for grade school students (once the students reach high school, they need to buy their own books)
- The passing grade for the students to proceed to the next grade is 60% (for national examinations)
- School days are usually shorter in Mexico especially for primary levels and high school levels because some children are already working or helping their parents in the morning; some students can only come to school in the afternoon. Schooling for public

schools starts in September until June of the following year.

- Public schools are usually underfunded by the government due to corruption especially in remote places.
- Most children of expats are not studying in public schools due to many disadvantages in its school system. Some who are already quite fluent in Spanish are the only ones who usually attend school in the morning but they are still home schooled by their parents in the afternoon.

Private Schools

- There are lots of private schools in Mexico but these institutions are usually found in large cities in the country
- Before considering any private schools, make sure that it is accredited under Mexico's Ministry of Public Education

- The quality of education in private schools will vary, which is why it's ideal to visit the school first to check the academic curriculum being offered to students, and possibly meet with the teachers to see if it's suitable for you as a parent, and for your children.

- Many private schools offers bilingual education, have broader curriculum, teaches Spanish and also English, and some are also internationally accredited.

- Before enrolling your kids, make sure that you meet the school's requirements. The requirements generally include a copy of your child's birth certificate, previous school records, identification of both the parents and the child as well as immigration visas. The child should also have completed the previous year in his/her former school, and must pass examinations/interviews of the school to qualify.

International Schools

- International schools in Mexico are the top choices of foreign parents because their child will receive a world – class education, and be able to attend any universities anywhere in the world including their home country should the parents decide to move back.

- The international schools in Mexico are mostly in capital cities in the country like Guadalajara, Mexico City, and Monterrey.

- Most international schools tuition fees' are quite expensive compared to private schools especially the elite ones. You can enroll your kids in an American school, English school, and Japanese school as well as German and French international schools.

Universities/ Colleges

- If your children is about to go to college or is already in college, you can enroll them in any universities in Mexico provided that they meet the grade requirements of the university, and that they qualify for their chosen degrees.

- A Bachelor's degree lasts usually for 4 years just like in most countries (unless the degree will need a licensure exam). For those expats wishing to continue

their studies in Mexico, you can enroll for a post –
graduate degree; a Master's degree usually takes
about 2 years while a Doctoral degree takes 3 years.

- Aside from the Bachelor's degree and post - graduate
  degrees, students can also take a Higher Technician
  certificate. This is for those people who cannot
  continue their college studies but who want to train in
  becoming a skilled worker/professional in specific
  fields.

- Most foreign students enroll in Centro de Enseñanza
  para Extranjeros located in Mexico City. The
  university is accredited by UNAM or the National
  Autonomous University of Mexico. Aside from
  diploma courses, you can also learn intensive
  language courses, art and literature courses, technical
  courses, and other subjects. The tuition fee for expats
  is much higher compared to Mexican students.

School/University Fees in Mexico

The tuition fees and other school fees included will greatly vary depending on where you enroll your child. Of course, you'll also need to add in the expenses for transportation, student's allowance, school supplies etc. The usual fee you'll need to pay includes but is not limited to the following:

- Monthly Tuition Fee
- First – Time Admission Fee
- Reinscription fees (annually)
- Student funds for activities/ after – school programs
- Textbooks

Recommended International Schools and Universities in Mexico for Expats

International Schools

- The American School Foundation
  <http://www.asf.edu.mx>
- The Edron Academy
  <http://www.edron.edu.mx>
- Instituto Thomas Jefferson
  <http://itj.edu.mx/>
- Greengates
  <http://www.greengates.edu.mx>
- Lancaster School
  <http://www.lancaster.edu.mx>
- Wingate School
  <http://www.wingateschool.mx>
- Peterson Schools
  <http://www.peterson.edu.mx>

Universities (with international programs and accreditation)

- Instituto Tecnologico de Estudios Superiores de Monterrey

  <http://www.itesm.mx>

- Universidad de las Americas, Puebla

  <http://www.udlap.mx/englishversion/>

- Universidad Iberoamericana

  <http://www.ibero.edu.mx>

- Instituto Tecnologico Autonomo de Mexico

  <http://www.itam.mx>

Chapter Eight: Taxes & Banking in Mexico

Benjamin Franklin, one of America's founding fathers famously said: *"The only thing certain in this world are death and taxes."* Even if you leave your home country, you still have to pay taxes in any country you choose to live in, including Mexico! As an expat in Mexico, the government will take money from your pocket through an income tax (if you're an employee/worker), property tax, and business tax. Even if you're already retired or just someone travelling in

Mexico, one way or another you'll have to incur certain taxes like the Value Added Tax every time you pay for goods or buy stuff.

It's important to note however, that as a foreigner the rules for paying taxes in Mexico, and the amount will be quite different and probably even less than what you pay in your home country which is one of the reasons why many expats also move here so that they can save more money by paying less tax. This is also advantageous for people who'll be doing business in the country because they can possibly minimize their tax obligations. It's probably best that if you're an expat looking to build a business in Mexico, you should consult a tax specialist or accountant so that you can choose the best option when it comes to declaring taxes for your business.

This chapter will give you an overview of the kinds of taxes you need to pay as a foreign national, and all the basics about tax paying in Mexico. We'll also cover how the banking system works in the country, the financial services available, the banks to choose from as well as the payment systems in place.

Taxation in Mexico

If you're a foreigner who is employed in Mexico, or someone who runs a business or is self – employed, rent out your property to a local or tourists, and if you have an interest bearing investments/bank account, you most likely need to file a Mexican tax return. Any form of income stream or business endeavor is required to pay out taxes to the Mexican government.

In this section, we'll take a look at the most common types of taxes you need to file if you're an expat in Mexico.

Income Taxes

Just like in many countries, you'll need to pay an income tax if you are an employee or engaged in some form of work that earns you a fixed income (there are some exceptions to this rule) but generally if you earn a living either through professional corporate work or as a self – employed individual, you need to file an income tax.

The income tax rate will vary from one individual to another depending on how much you earn per month or in a year. It will also depend on certain deductions of the company you work for. The tax rates of Mexican nationals ranges from 1.92% (low income earners) up to 35% (high income earners). For non – residents or expats usually pay a somewhat higher income tax around 15% to 30% unless of course your income is very low, then you may be exempted. A corporate tax in Mexico is around 30% (fixed rate) at the time of this writing.

The table below will show you the 2017 national income rates for <u>non – resident expats</u> in Mexico:

Earnings	Tax Rates
0 to 125,900 MXN	With Tax Exemption
125,900 to 1,000,000 MXN	15%

1,000,001 and above MXN	30%
Local Taxes (depends on the city/municipality/state	1% to 3%

Property Taxes

Foreign nationals who purchased a real estate property will need to pay 3 kinds of property taxes but it's very low compared to countries like USA and Canada or countries in Europe. The 3 types of property taxes you need to pay are:

- Acquisition Tax
- Annual Property Tax
- Capital Gains Tax

Acquisition Tax

- This is the first ever tax that will be collected once you closed the deal in your property.
- The acquisition tax is 2% and must be paid in cash or Mexican peso

- This is collected on behalf of the state or local municipality where the property is located.

Annual Property Tax (*Predial*)

- The annual property tax is what you owe to the municipality where your property is located, obviously it's a separate tax that you have to pay aside from the acquisition tax or once you acquire the property. You'll have to pay the local government again once a year.

- The annual property tax should be paid personally at the local municipal office. Sometimes the municipality sends bills but often times it can get lost because the mailing system is not that reliable, so make sure that you do your due diligence.

- It should also be paid in cash, and if you wanted to avail a discount make sure that you pay up early.

- Property tax usually costs just about US$100 both for houses and condominiums; although you may need to pay more if the property is large. The tax is also set by the local government or municipality where your property exists.

- If you acquire a property in a remote area, you might need to only pay less than $100 (except for beach front properties or possibly near tourist spots).

Capital Gains Tax

- Upon selling your property, you'll need to pay a capital gain tax or locally known as Impuesto Sobre la Renta.

- You have two options when paying the capital gains tax; you can choose a more favorable option. It's either you pay 20% of the declared value of the transaction or 28% to 30% of the net gain (less of the renovations made to the house, the commissions paid to agents as well as other allowable expenses.

- When computing for property taxes especially the capital gains tax, make sure that you get a Notario Publico or a lawyer specializing in taxation.

Value Added Tax

Last but definitely not the least is the Value Added Tax (VAT) or sales tax. Regardless if you're a low, average or high income earner, you will have to pay these taxes one way or another simply because you are a consumer, so you don't have any other choice. This is applied once you buy any goods or services – which is if you think about it, almost everything you need to function in your day to day life.

The value added tax in almost all of Mexico is about 16%, while the sales tax in border areas is about 11%. Every time you buy something, just look at your receipt to see how much you paid for the VAT.

Corporate Tax

Aside from income taxes, companies and corporations should also pay a corporate tax. Shareholders may be entitled to some tax benefits or exemptions. However, if the shares revenue of the company was not accounted when they paid their income tax, they'll have to pay another 35% tax on the shared sum. Aside from these, the owners should also pay a Federal income tax. Do take note that there can be certain tax exemptions like the net income of the company.

How to Register as a Taxpayer

As an expat, you need to register in the Federal Register of Taxpayers or FRT within 10 days of your arrival in Mexico. You can also do it online or go directly to the office of Administración Local de Servicios al Contribuyente.

Here are the general documents you need to present so you can properly file your taxes:

- Birth certificate
- Proof of address (utility bill/s)
- Identification card or passport
- Online file number (if you registered online)

If you can't present such requirements, what you need to present is a procuration letter that is either referred by Notario Public or the Mexican fiscal department. You may need to also bring 2 witnesses and concerned companies to be officially named as their legal representative.

Once you've submitted the requirements, you'll then receive a copy of your application, a FRT tax ID and also a user guide. Your yearly income declaration depends on your status whether you're an employee, a businessman, or a professional. Some pay taxes once a year while others pay every month. If ever you change your status or work situations, you should make sure to notify the FRT because it can alter your fiscal duties.

FAQs about Paying Taxes

When should I pay my taxes?

People file their taxes every 30th of April at the Servicio de Administración Tributaria, no extensions allowed. Employers are also required to file taxes of their employees on a monthly basis depending on the amount of compensation paid. Employee taxes c/o employers should be paid on or before the 17th of the following month.

Non – residents are required to pay within 15 days upon receipt of their income. Expats and Mexicans alike are also required to file an annual income tax.

What about social securities?

Just like in most countries, the employers will take care of the social security taxes of their employees, so you won't have to worry about filing those. However, if you are an expat in Mexico but you're working for a foreign company, and not employed in any Mexican owned company, it's ideal that you consult with an accountant or tax expert/lawyer because you may need to personally pay for your social security taxes.

Will my foreign income be taxes in Mexico?

If you are already considered as a resident in Mexico, then you will be taxed on your worldwide income. But for non –

residents, you will only be taxed if the money you earn from services rendered came from Mexico or is provided in a Mexican territory.

I'm a US Expat, is there any way I can save on my taxes?

Yes, there are many forms of taxation that can be applied to not just American expats but also other foreigners that is both working and living in Mexico. There will be certain deductions, inclusions as well as credits in your American taxes. It is advisable that you talk to a tax expert on how you can save taxes, and also comply with Mexican fiscal obligations.

Financial Institutions and Banking in Mexico

There are many financial institutions in Mexico that caters both to local and foreign nationals. The banks offer a variety of financial services to individual clients as well corporations or business entities.

Banks in Mexico pretty much offer the same financial services just like in many banks around the world; they offer savings account, debit cards, credit cards, loans, investments, time deposits, and also function as a payment channel.

For foreigners or expats residing in Mexico, these are three types of account you can hold aside from the services aforementioned:

(Mexican) Peso Checking Account

If you have an interest – bearing accounts or a regular savings account, foreigners can hold a peso checking account that allows them to both manage the money and also earn income through bank interests. The minimum deposit starts at US$500 to US$1,000 (depends on the account type).

US Dollar Checking Account

These accounts are usually offered to corporations as well as US and Canadian foreigners. There'll be interest rates for such accounts but it is significantly lower than that being offered in the US. The minimum opening for this account also varies.

Certificate of Deposit

This is a type of account that gives an ROI to the investor because the money is being invested or traded in the market, and the returns are also fixed by the bank. Such accounts are only offered in Mexican Peso, and the minimum opening is relatively higher.

General Requirements for Expats in Opening a Bank Account

Here are the general requirements that you need to provide before you can open any account in a Mexican bank:

- Residence Visa
- Identification cards (ex: passport)
- Proof of address (ex: utility bills)
- 2 references
- Minimum deposit (depends on the type of account you want to open).

If you apply for a debit or credit card, it will usually take 3 banking days before you receive it along with your temporary passwords and usernames (should you choose to have an online account or depending on the type of account).

Top Banks in Mexico

Here is a list of the most popular banks in Mexico that also has branches in United States, Canada, Asia, Latin America, Middle East and also in Europe. An international bank is ideal especially if you're a foreigner travelling from one country to another.

- **Banamex** (has branches in Europe, USA, Canada, Asia, Middle East, Australia, South America)
- **BBVA Bancomer** (has branches in USA, Spain)
- **Bank of America** (has branches in Europe, USA, Canada, Asia, Middle East, Australia, South America)
- **HSBC** (has branches in Europe, USA, Canada, Asia, Middle East, Australia, Africa)

- **Santander** (has branches in Europe, USA, Canada, Asia, South America, Australia)
- **Scotiabank** (has branches in Europe, USA, Canada, Asia, South America, Australia)

Tips for Expats when doing banking in Mexico

- Mexican banks are usually open from 9 AM - 4 PM; some banks are open on Saturdays from 10 AM - 2 PM.
- Large sum of cash deposits may be subject to tax rates except fund transfers and checks.
- Withdrawals from other bank's ATM comes with charges; some ATMs may not accept ATM cards of other banks.
- Some banks like HSBC, Santander, Banorte, and Scotiabank may require an expat to be in the country for a minimum of 6 months to a year before you can open a bank account.
- Banks may ask you to present your residential visa, certificate from your school (if you're an expat

student), and business credentials (if you're a foreign entrepreneur).

Reference for Financial Institutions in Mexico

Here's a list of the financial institutions that can be a useful reference when it comes to dealing with financial matters in Mexico:

Mexican Central Bank (Bank of Mexico): this institution is the mother of all banks in the country. It regulates all banking activities, protects consumers, and also controls the banking, and credit sectors. It also publishes weekly statistics relating to the economy, exchange rates and the likes.

Bur de Credito: This is the National Credit Bureau of Mexico where you can inquire about credit policies of banks or other matters related to credit or loans.

Profeco: it is an institution in Mexico that functions as the national consumer watchdog. They protect consumers, regulates financial services and products of banks and credit institutions as well. You can file a complaint here whether you're a resident or not if you think you have been misled.

Chapter Nine: Healthcare in Mexico

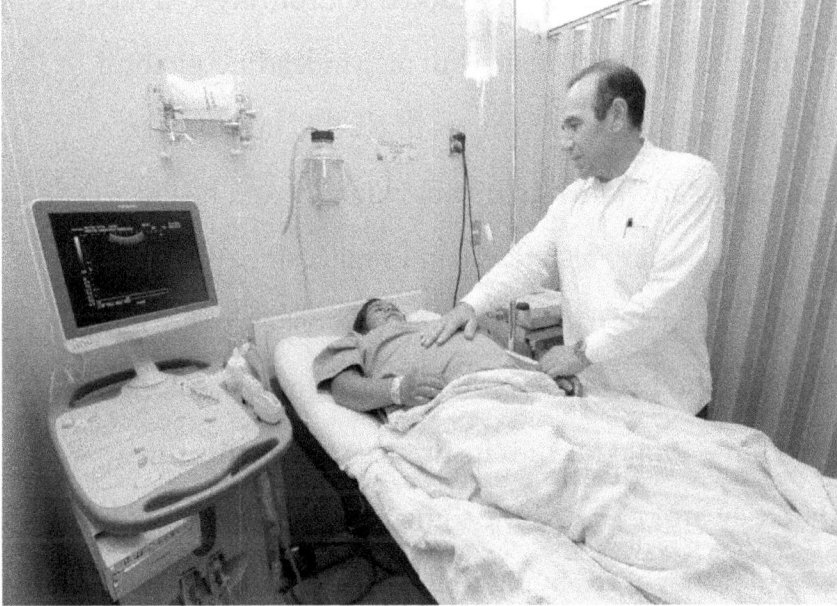

Another major reason why foreign nationals like to move in Mexico is because of its high standard yet very affordable healthcare services. The healthcare in Mexico is outstanding; every city has its own medical facilities and services that are deemed world – class in terms of its quality. You can fine many private clinics, private and public hospitals as well as about over 4,400 healthcare institutions that serves both locals and expats alike.

The doctors and medical professionals are also top – notch; most of them have studied and/or received medical training not just in Mexico but also in leading medical institutions in other countries like USA, Europe, and Canada. Many Mexican doctors, nurses, and health professionals are also fluent in English since most of them have studied abroad. According to most expats residing in Mexico who have received health treatments especially those who have availed health insurances or benefits, they said that they are receiving the same healthcare quality as one would if they were living in the US or Europe but for a much cheaper price.

Expats residing in Mexico are usually availing such treatments/consultations from private healthcare institutions in order to avoid the long lines in public hospitals or clinics, but the quality of service in these public health institutions are still excellent. Perhaps the only major difference between private and public hospitals is that the latter is only offering basic accommodation to the patients if ever they were admitted, and of course as with most countries, private hospitals in terms of facilities and equipment are still relatively better than public hospitals. If ever you are admitted, your relatives are usually not permitted to stay in the hospital.

This chapter will cover everything you need to know about healthcare in Mexico for foreign nationals as well as those who are planning to retire in the country for good.

How is the Healthcare Sector Being Funded in Mexico?

Mexico's regulatory body in terms of healthcare is called the Ministry of Health or locally known as Secretaria de Salud. Each state in the country also has its own autonomous health regulatory board known as Servicios Estates de Salud but these entities are still under the Ministry of Health. These are the institutions that are assigned in providing medical care to people who do not have health insurance or those who can't afford it. The national health fund is called Seguro Popular de Salud.

The funding mainly comes from employees and employers in Mexico through their contributions in the Social Security Fund, and in return workers can have access to health services if need be. This also applies to expats who are permitted to work and reside in the country.

Healthcare for Expats

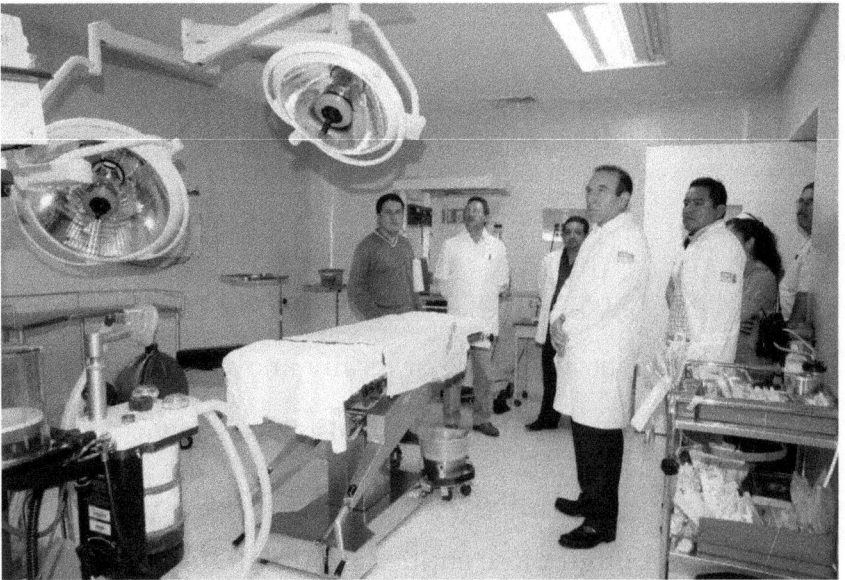

Foreign nationals working or residing in Mexico have the right to receive a health service under the IMSS program. However, it depends if the organization or company you work for registered you for the health service.

If you need to register on your own, the process could be rather complicated; here are the general documents you may need to submit.

- Passport
- Proof of working permit or residential visa
- Proof of residence
- Birth certificate (must be translated into Spanish)
- Marriage certificate (if applicable)
- Medical history (usually a questionnaire and medical reports)

The main advantage of registering under the IMSS program is that you will get covered for healthcare services in cases of emergencies or illnesses. After being approved and granted, you'll be issued a health card that you can present whenever you need to avail a healthcare or consult a medical professional. Most public hospitals offer low – cost consultation fees and treatments compare to private hospitals especially for people who are not covered by insurance.

If you are covered by a health insurance, you can then reimburse up to 80% of your medical expenses but it will vary depending on the terms and conditions of your insurance. You might also need to make an upfront payment for services you are charged for but you can file it for reimbursement.

Health Insurance for Expats

It's highly recommended that as you avail a local health insurance especially if you're planning to move in Mexico with your family. You should also have travel insurance regardless of your nationality so that you're always covered in case anything happens to you in a foreign country including Mexico.

It's important to note, however, that most medical facilities or hospitals in Mexico don't accept health insurances provided by international institutions. So if ever you have a health insurance from other countries, it will not be accepted and will not cover you in Mexico. If ever you got hospitalized or would need any treatment, you have no choice but to pay in cash especially if you're not registered under the IMSS program. What you can do is to file for a reimbursement if you have a health insurance that is based in other countries.

Lots of expats especially Americans avail an international health insurance before they move out of the country so that they can be covered in any country they reside or travel into, but unfortunately, that kind of policy is not applicable in Mexico. Expats are not provided any free treatment under Mexico's medical system and it does not recognize any insurance policies issued by providers overseas. This is why getting registered under the IMSS program is really beneficial as well as acquiring a health insurance from a Mexican health provider.

If ever your insurance provider in your home country is claiming that it is valid and effective overseas, then make sure to check the policies, the requirements, the duration, the possible fees, as well as the hospitals, treatments, facilities, and professionals that it will cover before moving to the country.

Most expats in Mexico are covered by IMSS through the companies they worked for, and they also availed an insurance plan from a Mexican health provider, some even have insurance from international companies, so just decide what will best suit you, your budget, and your possible needs.

Here are some facts and tips when applying for a health insurance in Mexico:

- Private health insurances usually have two major plans; comprehensive coverage and the catastrophic coverage.

- Many expats and even locals in Mexico are availing a comprehensive coverage simply because it generally covers everything health related including hospitalization costs, consultations, medicines, and other smaller expenses. As compared to catastrophic coverage where it only covers major treatments or emergencies.

- Many factors will come into play with regards to your insurance, the premium charged will usually be based upon your age, health risks, medical history, lifestyle, and the plan you choose.

- The average insurance premium that you need to pay every year starts from MXN 21,500 up to MXN 390,300 or US$1,100 to US$20,000. This can greatly vary depending on the insurance company you signed up for. Make sure to compare plans and prices of different companies before deciding.

- There are many insurance providers in Mexico that has agreements to private and public hospitals or clinics that a patient will not need to pay once discharged or treated. However, the usual norm is that the patients pay upfront, and they just file a reimbursement in their insurance companies. The reimbursement filing can be quite confusing; you may need to file the receipts/invoices and other forms upon claiming your reimbursement and it will also take a few days or so before you can claim it.

Pharmacy and Medications in Mexico

In Mexico, the healthcare services are much cheaper than in most countries but not the medicines. Medicines especially antibiotics and premium brands are very expensive, so make sure that your insurance plan also covers medication expenses or at least a percentage of it for you to be save a significant amount of cash.

Pharmacies in Mexico abound not just in major cities but also in remote places, you can purchase medicines over - the – counter easily. However, some medicines may not be available in remote places.

Healthcare for Expat Retirees

If you're already a retiree (specifically those over 60 years old), and you didn't availed any form of health insurance when you were younger, you definitely will need to pay a higher premium price for insurance or health coverage (if it's still available).

Private health insurance companies in Mexico and in other countries usually have a cut off for new policies. There are still a few health providers that offer new health care policies for those who are 65 years old and above but it will already be very expensive as this is the age where illness and various health problems usually arises plus they won't cover your pre – existing conditions. An insurance company called BUPA Mexico is one example where they still offer policies but only until 74 years old and 11 months of age.

You can also choose to sign up for the IMSS program, and just pay around US$360 a year/person so that you can at least have a backup. The main advantage of retiring in

Mexico in terms of healthcare is that even if you're not registered to an IMSS program or doesn't have any form of insurance from local providers, the cost of health treatments or hospitalizations is way cheaper compared to other countries like United States, and in the UK so you can definitely afford it.

Chapter Ten: Preparing for Your Relocation in Mexico

Once you or your spouse/children have decided to move to Mexico, and have weighed all the pros and cons in all the important things you need to consider, then it's time to prepare for your relocation. You will have to deal with a plethora of things, and will also need a substantial amount of time especially in terms of organizing the documents that you'll need before you move there.

You and your family will need to do careful planning before, and after you moved out of your home country, and moved into your new home in Mexico.

Your relocation plan will highly depend on your own living situations but key factors such as your status (whether you're single or married), age, purpose, and financial capacity will definitely influence the complexity of your relocation. Those who are young, single, and working individuals will have a less complicated situation when it comes to moving into another country compared to those who will move with their families and those expat retirees who may need someone to look after them.

This chapter will focus on all the most important things you need to consider about 3 months ahead of your move. This is a practical checklist for you and your family so that you'll know what to do, and will have enough time to take care of your unique situations, and so that you won't miss out anything. There are many aspects when relocating to a foreign country; this pre – moving checklist will guide you at the different planning stage of your relocation including how to legally move to Mexico with your family as well as your possessions.

Mexico Relocation Checklist

3 months Before the Move

Here's a breakdown of all the items that needs to be organized 3 months prior to your departure date:

Legal Matters/ Documents:

- **Passport:** must have at least one year validity (especially if you're going to apply for a Mexican resident visa). If it's already expired or about to expire, then renew it as soon as possible before submitting it to the Mexican Consulate in order for your application to be processed without delay.

- **Travel Documents:** you and your family must have valid passports, and have already applied for a resident visa or for a working permit. If you're an employee, chances are your employer will be in charge of acquiring the residence visa/working permit for you (and your family). If not, then make sure that you have all the requirements necessary to qualify, and are eligible of working, doing business, or retiring in Mexico.

- **Driver's License:** You don't need to get an international driver's license. If you need to get a driver's license in Mexico, you can just apply in the country. The requirements, fees, and process will vary from one state to another. Just make sure you have all the necessary documents like residency visa/working permit/passport etc.

Household

- **Electrical Appliances:** make sure that you have a checklist of all the appliances you want to take with you once you make the move. Gadgets like smart phones, laptops, Ipads, TV, and refrigerator may or may not have the same voltage in Mexico, so you probably need to buy a transformer or an adapter. However, also consider if you can just leave it behind and purchase new items in Mexico especially the big – ticket items like the TV and refrigerator. Most European and Asian electrical furniture will not work in Mexico, and relocating such big items may not be a good idea because it can get destroyed or damaged during shipment.

- **Other Household Items:** It's now time to consider the home items you'll need to take with you and leave behind. Chances are, you won't really need a lot of them once you make the move, so now is the time to consider doing a garage sale, or just hand it over to your relatives and friends.

- **Pets:** Not all pets can be taken to Mexico. Usual pets like dogs and cats will definitely need a permit, and you have to also ensure that your pet has all the required vaccinations and medical papers so that they can legally go with you to Mexico. Usually, what you'll need is a health certificated issued by a licensed vet in your home country, and your pet should also be vaccinated for rabies at least 15 days before arrival. Other animals like snakes, rabbits, birds, and the likes will most likely need a special import permit. Make sure to ask proper authorities about the requirements of moving in with your pets.

Vehicles

- This doesn't only apply to just cars, but also to motorcycles, boats, trucks or other vehicles you might own. If you live in USA, you can most likely move them with you, but if you're living in Europe, Asia or other far – off continents then you have no choice but to leave it there. However, you can still of course ship them overseas if you can afford it. Prepare now to sell them especially once your Mexican visas are approved.

Real Estate

- **House/ Properties:** By this time, you should have already thought about what you will do with your existing house or properties. You can rent it out, sell it up or just leave it idle. Make sure to get a real estate broker or someone who you trust to either sell or manage your property. If you're just renting, then make sure that you check your lease contracts, settle all your payments, and also inform your landlord. Never ever sell your property or give notice on your rented home until you're sure that your Mexican visas are already approved.

- **Accommodation upon arrival:** Make sure that you already have a place to stay once you arrive in Mexico. If you're going to temporary stay at a hotel or rent out a place, then make sure that you're already booked ahead of time, or you have already informed your landlord as to when you're going to arrive. If you bought a property, then make sure that you can already move there once you arrive, and always stay in touch with your broker or real estate agent in Mexico.

2 months Before the Move

Here's a breakdown of all the items that needs to be organized 2 months prior to your departure date:

- **Compare Quotes of Moving Companies:** Now that you have decided what to bring and leave behind, it's time to select the right moving company that will take care of your personal items to your new place in Mexico. If you are in North America or Latin America, then it'll be most likely delivered by road, but if you live in far – off continents, you should decide if your stuff is going to be shipped via sea or air. Check the quotes of different companies, and pick the established ones so that you're guaranteed that your personal things are in good hands.

- **Importing Your Things to Mexico:** personal items like clothes, light gadgets, books etc. are duty – free, but big items like electrical appliances are subject to a duty limit and taxes. It's best that you travel light, and just let the moving company bring such big ticket items to you because they are experts when it comes to dealing with customs. It's also wise to just leave the big things behind at least until you get settled, and then just have them shipped to your home. You also have the option to rent out a storage room in Mexico for your big items so make sure you have arranged it before moving.

- **Select or Arrange Schools for Your Children:** By this time you should have already selected what school your children is going to go into, and ensure that the requirements are met. You need to also secure a copy of important documents from your child's previous school.

- **Airline Reservations/ Boat Tickets/ Travel by Road:** If you and your family are already granted a Mexican visa, then it's also time to book a flight, or buy ferry tickets, or get your car ready. Make reservations ahead of time so you can choose the best options, and be able to save time and money, and also avoid any delays.

- **Change of Address:** You should also make sure that you informed all the organizations associated with you that you're going to change address soon. If you don't have a permanent address in Mexico, then just arrange a holding or forwarding address.

- **Start packing things up:** It's best that you already start segregating the items you'll bring with you as well as the items that will be shipped to you once you move. Time to buy those boxes!

- **Gather all the important documents:** Make sure that you have a file of all the personal documents you'll need once you enter the country. This includes birth certificate (of you and your children), marriage certificate (if applicable), qualification certificates, stock/investment certificates, bank statements, identification card etc.

- **Arrange Financial Matters and Tax Affairs:** It's now time to close your local bank accounts, pay off debts/loans, fix your mortgage, and cancel your existing credit cards, checking accounts etc. in your home country. By this time, you (and your spouse) should have calculated your household expenses each month, and arrange the cost of living. If you are a retiree, then ensure that your pension papers, properties, and other investments/accounts are handled and organized. Upon entry in Mexico, you'll need to present your proof of income, bank statements, investment certificates, and other related financial documents to see if you can sustain a living in Mexico aside from your visas, permits, and other travel documents. Make sure that you have also arranged your tax plans before you moved to Mexico. Consult an accountant and contact tax authorities in your home country to ensure that everything is smooth before you move out.

- **Arrange your Voting Rights:** Unless you're already a naturalized Mexican, you can still vote during elections in your home country. Check with your local government on how to register voting abroad.

1 month Before the Move

Here's a breakdown of all the items that needs to be organized 1 month prior to your departure date:

- **Passports, Travel Documents, Visas:** Your travel documents, passports, and visas should all be ready by now.

- **House/ Properties:** By this time, you should have arrangements as to how your house or properties will be transferred to the new owner (if you already sold it), and the final preparations for your new tenant (if you rent it out). It's wise to hire the services of a realtor to take care of the final housing arrangements on your behalf. You should have also hired a caretaker for your house while you're away if you don't want to sold it or rent it out before completely vacating it.

- **Personal Items:** You should have already sold or given away all your unwanted goods a month before your move. Or if not, the items should already be in storage either in your home country or have arranged one in Mexico once it arrives.

- **Inform the organizations/people of your move:** Make sure to contact the organizations you're associated in including banks, local government, utility companies, memberships/clubs, your

children's school/clubs, subscriptions, delivery
systems, financial institutions, insurance provider,
vehicle registries, tax authorities, property agencies,
accountant, lawyer, doctor, your friends, other
relatives, and all the people associated with you and
your family.

- **Arrange your medical records, health documents,
  and prescriptions:** Make sure to have a copy of you
  and your family's medical certificates, medical history
  as well as prescriptions from your doctor. It's also
  ideal that you and your family have a last
  medical/dental check-up before you leave.

- **Clear out food storages and kitchen items:** prepare
  and make a checklist of the food items you need to
  consume or defrost. Prepare to clear out cupboards
  and dry goods as well including your cellar, and
  basement if ever you have other things/food stored in

there, it's now time to consume them, give them away or dispose it.

- **Confirm tickets, reservations, permits, and other arrangements you've made:** Make sure that your moving company, real estate agent, service providers, transportation arrangements, and other important things are already settled and ready to go.

1 Week Before the Move

Here's a breakdown of all the items that needs to be organized 1 week prior to your departure date:

- **Prepare to Vacate Your House:** Everything that needs to be sold or donated must already be done; your freezer, cellar, food storage must already be emptied out. All the items you're going to leave behind should either be gone or put into storage. Your other pending items like laundry should already be picked up; your plants should be taken care of or given away to neighbors. It's also best to stay with your nearby relatives, friends or hotel if you're bed is already packed up.

- **Get your bags/luggage ready:** Make sure that you and your family are already packed up; this includes the things you'll bring to the airport with you, and the luggage containing your personal items. Make sure that you have enough clothes once you arrive in Mexico while you're waiting for your other stuff to be shipped.

The Day of Moving

- **Empty the House:** You should already be either out of the house (especially if you hired a professional cleaning service so that they'll have time to clean it) or in a hotel or nearby friend so you can have time to relax as well.

- **Final Meter Readings:** Take one last final meter readings of your electricity, water, gas or telephone. Unplug or close all the circuits before you leave.

- **Do a final check of the house:** After everything is moved out, check the property one last time, and well, say your goodbyes!

- **Double check your travel documents, money, and other necessities:** This is the most important part! You need to make sure that all your travel documents, visas, permits etc. are ready and can be easily access to avoid any hassles.

Basic Travel Essentials

Before this book comes to an end, we'll give you the basic travel essentials that you need to know before making the move to Mexico. It's very important that you have an idea of what to expect so that you'll know how to go about in this beautiful country. We'll give you a quick rundown of the things you need to know while travelling in Mexico, and also include a list of the top tourist destinations, and the places where you can get the most authentic Mexican cuisines.

We hope this book helped you in preparing for your move to Mexico, and provided you with the knowledge you need on how to become an expat in a foreign country. Most importantly, we hoped that this book has encouraged you to try out a different culture, and consider settling in a new environment like Mexico for you to not just appreciate the Mexican way of life but also your own national heritage.

Mexico Basic Essentials

Here's a quick run – down of the basic essentials when travelling to Mexico:

- **Capital City:** Mexico City
- **Population:** 129 Million (as of 2017)
- **Government:** Federal Republic; democratically elected president
- **Current President:** President Enrique Peña Nieto (2012 – present). Next election is 2018 (at the time of this writing).
- **Religion:** 90% Roman Catholic; open to all religions
- **Currency:** Mexican Peso (MXN/ Mex$)

- **Language:** Spanish; English
- **Time Zone:** GMT - 6, - 7 and - 8 with daylight saving, and GMT - 7 all year round
- **Electricity:** 130 volts, 60Hz (two – pin flat blade plug)
- **ATMs/Money:** Visa, Master Card, American Express are widely accepted; traveller's cheques and foreign currencies are also accepted in major shops/restaurants

- **General Entry Requirements:**
    - Valid Passport
    - Tourist Visa/ Residence Visas/Permits
    - Return Tickets
    - Hotel bookings/reservations
    - Letter of invitation (if applicable)
    - Other travel documents (bank statements; proof of sufficient funds etc.)

- **Climate:** Usually hot and humid all year round in most areas; highlands are drier but freezing from December to February. Rainfall is scarce.

- **Tipping:** at least 10 – 15% tip for local waiters/bars/restaurants if service charge is not yet included. At least 15 – 20% if you are dining in international establishments.

- **Communication:**
  - International code of Mexico is +52 on the telephone; outgoing code is 00 plus the country code you're going to call
  - Area Codes: (0)55 (Mexico City); (0)744 (Acapulco); (0)998 (Cancun)
  - Internet access, public Wi–Fi and mobile networks are widely available in the country.
  - Emergency Numbers: 060; 080

- **Important Dates**
    - **Jan 6:** 3 Wise Men Day
    - **Feb 2:** The Candelaria Virgin Day
    - **Feb 5: Day of Constitution**
    - **Mar 21: Birthday of Benito Juarez**
    - **May 1: Labor Day**
    - **May 5: The Battle of Puebla**
    - **Sept 1:** Dia del Informe (State of the Nation Address)
    - **Sept 15:** Grito de Dolores
    - **Sept 16:** Independence Day
    - **Nov 2:** All Soul's Day
    - **Nov 20:** Revolution Day
    - **Dec 12:** Feast of the Virgin Mary of Guadalupe

PHOTO REFERENCES

Foreword Page Photo by user Geraint Rowland via
Flickr.com,
https://www.flickr.com/photos/geezaweezer/7983004328/

Page 1 Photo by user Antony Stanley via Flickr.com,
https://www.flickr.com/photos/antonystanley/2105552839/

Page 6 Photo by user Justin Vidamo via Flickr.com,
https://www.flickr.com/photos/21160499@N04/14204603663/

Page 17 Photo by user ManuCarrillo via Pixabay.com,
https://pixabay.com/en/danzon-dance-mexican-couple-
2439132/

Page 27 Photo by user Kaufdex via Pixabay.com,
https://pixabay.com/en/mexico-flag-international-2697062/

Page 35 Photo by user Khe via Flickr.com,
https://www.flickr.com/photos/khedara/4644306408/

Page 54 Photo by user Walkerssk via Pixabay.com,
https://pixabay.com/en/mexico-mexico-city-palace-art-
2014178/

Page 57 Photo by user providercariou via Pixabay.com, https://pixabay.com/en/mexico-yucatan-chichen-itza-2898220/

Page 60 Photo by user Wiktor via Pixabay.com, https://pixabay.com/en/hotel-caribs-mexico-yucatan-2869222/

Page 68 Photo by user Walkerssk via Pixabay.com, https://pixabay.com/en/tulum-mexico-beach-beach-in-mexico-2006701/

Page 82 Photo by user Emilian Danaila via Pixabay.com, https://pixabay.com/en/mexico-cancun-sun-party-summer-2459387/

Page 87 Photo by user VV Nincic via Flickr.com, https://www.flickr.com/photos/blok70/25238052149/

Page 100 Photo by user iivangm via Flickr.com, https://www.flickr.com/photos/ivangm/8843545295/

Page 105 Photo by user VV Nincic via Flickr.com, https://www.flickr.com/photos/blok70/25280987269/

Page 112 Photo by user Russ Bowling via Flickr.com, https://www.flickr.com/photos/robphoto/2832591281/

Page 128 Photo by user Rick González via Flickr.com, https://www.flickr.com/photos/ricardogz10/27238259561/

Page 135 Photo by user Christian Frausto Bernal via Flickr.com, https://www.flickr.com/photos/cfrausto/199772879/

Page 144 Photo by user aaandrea via Flickr.com, https://pixabay.com/en/family-portrait-white-mexico-2432048/

Page 156 Photo by user Al Case via Flickr.com, https://www.flickr.com/photos/60035031@N06/14928182435/

Page 168 Photo by user Jerry "Woody" via Flickr.com, https://www.flickr.com/photos/woodysworld1778/4418226219/

Page 180 Photo by user Ell David via Flickr.com, https://www.flickr.com/photos/vegandavid/8370103575/

Page 187 Photo by user German Tenorio via Flickr.com, https://www.flickr.com/photos/germantenorio/8600730169/

Page 190 Photo by user German Tenorio via Flickr.com, https://www.flickr.com/photos/germantenorio/8600713465/

Page 200 Photo by user Martha Silva via Flickr.com, https://www.flickr.com/photos/marthax/328682590/

Page 218 Photo by user cgmely via Flickr.com, https://www.flickr.com/photos/110269355@N06/14800253169/

REFERENCES

"A Guide to Health Insurance In Mexico" ExpatFocus.com
http://www.expatfocus.com/c/aid=3952/articles/mexico/a-
guide-to-health-insurance-in-mexico/

"Can expats set up a business in Mexico?" The Yucatan
Times
http://www.theyucatantimes.com/2015/11/can-expats-set-up-
a-business-in-mexico/

"Cost of Living in Mexico" ExpatArrivals.com
http://www.expatarrivals.com/mexico/cost-of-living-in-
mexico

"Everything you need to know to make the most of your
money!" MoneyTis.com
https://moneytis.com/en/blog/living-abroad/how-to-open-a-
bank-account-in-mexico

"How to Relocate and Move to Mexico" Mexperience.com
https://www.mexperience.com/lifestyle/living-in-
mexico/moving-to-mexico/

"Living in Mexico: Q&A" Mexperience.com
https://www.mexperience.com/lifestyle/living-in-mexico/questions-and-answers/

"Mexico" WikiTravel.org
https://wikitravel.org/en/Mexico
"Mexico and Canada: the best calling, texting and roaming plans compared" WhistleOut.com
https://www.whistleout.com/CellPhones/Guides/mexico-and-canada-best-calling-texting-roaming-plans-compared

"Mexico: Banking" ExpatFocus.com
http://www.expatfocus.com/expatriate-mexico-banking

"Mexico Entry Requirements" Mexperience.com
https://www.mexperience.com/lifestyle/mexico-essentials/mexico-entry-requirements/

"Mexico Essentials" Mexperience.com
https://www.mexperience.com/lifestyle/mexico-essentials/

"Mexican Real Estate FAQs" BanderasNews.com
http://www.banderasnews.com/real-estate/frequent-questions.htm

"Mexico Real Estate: Where there's a will there's a way"
MexConnect.com
http://www.mexconnect.com/articles/322-mexico-real-estate-where-there-s-a-will-there-s-a-way

"Mexico: Utilities (Electricity, Gas, Water)"
ExpatFocus.com
http://www.expatfocus.com/expatriate-mexico-utilities

"Mexican Visas and Immigration" Mexperience.com
https://www.mexperience.com/lifestyle/living-in-mexico/visas-and-immigration/

"Schools and Education in Mexico" Mexperience.com
https://www.mexperience.com/lifestyle/living-in-mexico/schools-in-mexico/

"Tax system in Mexico" Expat.com
http://www.expat.com/en/guide/north-america/mexico/10732-tax-system-in-mexico.html

"Timeline and History Overview" Ducksters.com
http://www.ducksters.com/geography/country/mexico_history_timeline.php

"Where Do Mexico's 1 Million U.S. Expats Live?"
VivaTropical.com
https://vivatropical.com/mexico/where-do-mexicos-1-million-u-s-expats-live/

"Where the Expats Live in Mexico"
EverythingPlayadelCarmen.com
http://everythingplayadelcarmen.com/where-the-expats-live-in-mexico/

"Why Mexico Scores Big for Expat Families"
VivaTropical.com
https://vivatropical.com/mexico-is-great-for-expat-families

"Working in Mexico: Q&A" Mexperience.com
https://www.mexperience.com/lifestyle/working-in-mexico/questions-and-answers/

www.ingramcontent.com/pod-product-compliance
Lightning Source LLC
Chambersburg PA
CBHW071419090426
42737CB00011B/1510